I0157888

Thespis by Gilbert & Sullivan

or THE GODS GROWN OLD

Libretto by William S. Gilbert
Music by Arthur Sullivan

The partnership between William Schwenck Gilbert and Arthur Seymour Sullivan and their canon of Savoy Operas is rightly lauded by all lovers of comic opera the world over.

Gilbert's sharp, funny words and Sullivan's deliciously lively and hummable tunes create a world that is distinctly British in view but has the world as its audience.

Both men were exceptionally talented and gifted in their own right and wrote much, often with other partners, that still stands the test of time. However, together as a team they created Light or Comic Operas of a standard that have had no rivals equal to their standard, before or since. That's quite an achievement.

To be recognised by the critics is one thing but their commercial success was incredible. The profits were astronomical, allowing for the building of their own purpose built theatre – The Savoy Theatre.

Beginning with the first of their fourteen collaborations, Thespis in 1871 and travelling through many classics including The Sorcerer (1877), H.M.S. Pinafore (1878), The Pirates of Penzance (1879), The Mikado (1885), The Gondoliers (1889) to their finale in 1896 with The Grand Duke, Gilbert & Sullivan created a legacy that is constantly revived and admired in theatres and other media to this very day.

Index of Contents

Thespis or The Gods Grown Old was the first collaboration of Gilbert and Sullivan. It was written as a Christmas entertainment for John Hollingshead's Gaiety Theatre and premiered on December 26th 1871 and ran for 63 performances.

DRAMATIS PERSONAE
GODS
Jupiter, Aged Diety

Apollo, Aged Diety
Mars, Aged Diety
Diana, Aged Diety
Mercury
THESPIANS
Thespis
Sillimon
Timidon
Tipseion
Preposteros
Stupidas
Sparkeion
Nicemis
Pretteia
Daphne
Cymon

SCENES
ACT I - Ruined Temple on the Summit of Mount Olympus
ACT II - The same Scene, with the Ruins Restored

MUSICAL NUMBERS
ACT II
Throughout the night, the constellations (Women's Chorus, with Solo)
Oh, I'm the celestial drudge (Mercury)
Oh incident unprecedented (Mercury, Mars, Apollo, Diana, and Jupiter)
Here far away from all the world (Sparkeion and Nicemis)
Climbing over rocky mountain" (Chorus with Solos)
Picnic Waltz
I once knew a chap who discharged a function (Thespis)
Act I Finale: So that's arranged – you take my place, my boy (Ensemble)
ACT II
Of all symposia (Sillimon and Chorus)
Little maid of Arcadee (Sparkeion)
Olympus is now in a terrible muddle (Mercury)
You're Diana. I'm Apollo (Sparkeion, Daphne, Nicemis and Thespis)
Oh rage and fury, Oh shame and sorrow (Jupiter, Apollo, and Mars)
Act II Finale: We can't stand this (Ensemble)

ACT I

[Scene—The ruins of the The Temple of the Gods, on summit of Mount Olympus. Picturesque shattered columns, overgrown with ivy, etc. R. and L. with entrances to temple (ruined) R. Fallen columns on the stage. Three broken pillars 2 R.E. At the back of stage is the approach from the summit of the mountain.

This should be "practicable" to enable large numbers of people to ascend and descend. In the distance are the summits of adjacent mountains. At first all this is concealed by a thick fog, which clears presently. Enter (through fog) Chorus of Stars coming off duty as fatigued with their night's work]

CHORUS
Through the night, the constellations,
Have given light from various stations.
When midnight gloom falls on all nations,
We will resume our occupations.

SOLO
Our light, it's true, is not worth mention;
What can we do to gain attention.
When night and noon with vulgar glaring
A great big moon is always flaring.

[During chorus, enter DIANA, an elderly goddess. She is carefully wrapped up in cloaks, shawls, etc. A hood is over her head, a respirator in her mouth, and galoshes on her feet. During the chorus, she takes these things off and discovers herself dressed in the usual costume of the Lunar Diana, the goddess of the moon.

DIANA [shuddering]
Ugh. How cold the nights are. I don't know how
it is, but I seem to feel the night air a good deal more than I
used to. But it is time for the sun to be rising. [Calls] Apollo.

APOLLO [within]
Hollo.

DIANA
I've come off duty—it's time for you to be getting up.

[Enter APOLLO. He is an elderly "buck" with an air of assumed juvenility and is dressed in dressing gown and smoking cap.

APOLLO [yawning]
I shan't go out today. I was out yesterday and the day before and I want a little rest. I don't know how it is, but I seem to feel my work a great deal more than I used to.

DIANA
I am sure these short days can't hurt you. Why you don't rise til six and you're in bed again by five; you should have a turn at my work and see how you like that—out all night.

APOLLO
My dear sister, I don't envy you—though I remember when I did—but that was when I was a younger sun. I don't think I'm quite well. Perhaps a little change of air will do me good. I've a mind to show myself in London this winter. They'll be very glad to see me. No. I shan't go out today. I shall send them

this fine, thick wholesome fog and they won't miss me. It's the best substitute for a blazing sun—and like most substitutes, nothing at all like the real thing.

[Fog clears away and discovers the scene described. Hurried music. MERCURY shoots up from behind precipice at the back of stage. He carries several parcels afterwards described. He sits down, very much fatigued.]

MERCURY
Home at last. A nice time I've had of it.

DIANA
You young scamp you've been out all night again. This is the third time you've been out this week.

MERCURY
Well you're a nice one to blow me up for that.

DIANA
I can't help being out all night.

MERCURY
And I can't help being down all night. The nature of Mercury requires that he should go down when the sun sets, and rise again when the sun rises.

DIANA
And what have you been doing?

MERCURY
Stealing on commission. There's a set of false teeth and a box of Life Pills for Jupiter—an invisible peruke and a bottle of hair dye—that's for Apollo—a respirator and a pair of galoshes—that's for Cupid—a full bottomed chignon, some auricomous fluid, a box of pearl-powder, a pot of rouge, and a hare's foot—that's for Venus.

DIANA
Stealing. You ought to be ashamed of yourself.

MERCURY
Oh, as the god of thieves I must do something to justify my position.

DIANA and APOLLO [contemptuously]
Your position.

MERCURY
Oh, I know it's nothing to boast of even on earth. Up here, it's simply contemptible. Now that you gods are too old for your work, you've made me the miserable drudge of Olympus—groom, valet, postman, butler, commissionaire, maid of all work, parish beadle, and original dustman.

APOLLO
Your Christmas boxes ought to be something considerable.

MERCURY

They ought to be but they're not. I'm treated abominably. I make everybody and I'm nobody. I go everywhere and I'm nowhere. I do everything and I'm nothing. I've made thunder for Jupiter, odes for Apollo, battles for Mars, and love for Venus. I've married couples for Humen and six weeks afterwards, I've divorced them for Cupid, and in return I get all the kicks while they pocket the halfpence. And in compensation for robbing me of the halfpence in question, what have they done for me.

APOLLO

Why they've—ha.ha.ha. they've made you the god of thieves.

MERCURY

Very self denying of them. There isn't one of them who hasn't a better claim to the distinction than I have.

Oh, I'm the celestial drudge,
For morning to night I must stop at it.
On errands all day I must trudge,
And stick to my work til I drop at it.
In summer I get up at one.
(As a good-natured donkey I'm ranked for it.)
then I go and I light up the sun.
And Phoebus Apollo gets thanked for it.
Well, well, it's the way of the world.
And will be through all its futurity.
Though noodles are baroned and earled,
There's nothing for clever obscurity.

I'm the slave of the Gods, neck and heels,
And I'm bound to obey, though I rate at 'em.
And I not only order their meals,
But I cook 'em and serve'em and wait at 'em.
Then I make all their nectar, I do.
(What a terrible liquor to rack us is.)
And whenever I mix them a brew,
Why all the thanksgivings are Bacchus's.
Well, well, it's the way of the world, etc.....

The reading and writing I teach.
And spelling-books many I've edited.
And for bringing those arts within reach,
That donkey Minerva gets credited.
Then I scrape at the stars with a knife,
And plate-powder the moon (on the days for it).
And I hear all the world and his wife
Awarding Diana the praise for it.
Well, well, it's the way of the world, etc....

[After song—very loud and majestic music is heard]

DIANA and MERCURY [looking off]
Why, who's this? Jupiter, by Jove.

[Enter JUPITER, an extremely old man, very decrepit, with very thin straggling white beard, he wears a long braided dressing gown, handsomely trimmed, and a silk night-cap on his head. MERCURY falls back respectfully as he enters.]

JUPITER
Good day, Diana. Ah, Apollo. Well, well, well, what's the matter? What's the matter?

DIANA
Why that young scamp Mercury says that we do nothing, and leave all the duties of Olympus to him. Will you believe it, he actually says that our influence on earth is dropping down to nil.

JUPITER
Well, well. Don't be hard on the lad. To tell you the truth, I'm not sure that he's far wrong. Don't let it go any further, but, between ourselves, the sacrifices and votive offerings have fallen off terribly of late. Why, I can remember the time when people offered us human sacrifices, no mistake about it, human sacrifices. Think of that.

DIANA
Ah. Those good old days.

JUPITER
Then it fell off to oxen, pigs, and sheep.

APOLLO
Well, there are worse things than oxen, pigs and sheep.

JUPITER
So I've found to my cost. My dear sir, between ourselves, it's dropped off from one thing to another until it has positively dwindled down to preserved Australian beef. What do you think of that?

APOLLO
I don't like it at all.

JUPITER
You won't mention it. It might go further.

DIANA
It couldn't fare worse.

JUPITER
In short, matters have come to such a crisis that there's no mistake about it—something must be done to restore our influence, the only question is, what?

MERCURY [Coming forward in great alarm. Enter MARS]
Oh incident unprecedented.
I hardly can believe it's true.

MARS
Why, bless the boy, he's quite demented.
Why, what's the matter, sir, with you?

APOLLO
Speak quickly, or you'll get a warming.

MERCURY
Why, mortals up the mount are swarming
Our temple on Olympus storming,
In hundreds—aye in thousands, too.

ALL
Goodness gracious
How audacious
Earth is spacious
Why come here?
Our impeding
Their proceeding
Were good breeding
That is clear.

DIANA
Jupiter, hear my plea.
Upon the mount if they light.
There'll be an end of me.
I won't be seen by daylight.

APOLLO
Tartarus is the place
These scoundrels you should send to—
Should they behold my face.
My influence there's an end to.

JUPITER [looking over precipice]
What fools to give themselves so much exertion

DIANA
A government survey I'll make assertion.

APOLLO
Perhaps the Alpine clubs their diversion.

MERCURY

They seem to be more like a "Cook's" excursion.

ALL
Goodness gracious, etc.

APOLLO
If, mighty Jove, you value your existence,
Send them a thunderbolt with your regards.

JUPITER
My thunderbolts, though valid at a distance,
Are not effective at a hundred yards.

MERCURY
Let the moon's rays, Diana, strike 'em flighty,
Make 'em all lunatics in various styles.

DIANA
My lunar rays unhappily are mighty
Only at many hundred thousand miles.

ALL
Goodness gracious, etc...

[Exeunt JUPITER, APOLLO, DIANA, and MERCURY into ruined temple]

[Enter SPARKEION and NICEMIS climbing mountain at back.]

SPARKEION
Here we are at last on the very summit, and we've left the others ever so far behind. Why, what's this?

NICEMIS
A ruined palace. A palace on the top of a mountain. I wonder who lives here? Some mighty kind, I dare say, with wealth beyond all counting who came to live up here—

SPARKEION
To avoid his creditors. It's a lovely situation for a country house though it's very much out of repair.

NICEMIS
Very inconvenient situation.

SPARKEION
Inconvenient.

NICEMIS
Yes, how are you to get butter, milk, and eggs up here? No pigs, no poultry, no postman. Why, I should go mad.

SPARKEION

What a dear little practical mind it is. What a wife you will make.

NICEMIS

Don't be too sure—we are only partly married—the marriage ceremony lasts all day.

SPARKEION

I have no doubt at all about it. We shall be as happy as a king and queen, though we are only a strolling actor and actress.

NICEMIS

It's very nice of Thespis to celebrate our marriage day by giving the company a picnic on this lovely mountain.

SPARKEION

And still more kind to allow us to get so much ahead of all the others. Discreet Thespis. [kissing her]

NICEMIS

There now, get away, do. Remember the marriage ceremony is not yet completed.

SPARKEION

But it would be ungrateful to Thespis's discretion not to take advantage of it by improving the opportunity.

NICEMIS

Certainly not; get away.

SPARKEION

On second thought the opportunity's so good it don't admit of improvement. There. [kisses her]

NICEMIS

How dare you kiss me before we are quite married?

SPARKEION

Attribute it to the intoxicating influence of the mountain air.

NICEMIS

Then we had better do down again. It is not right to expose ourselves to influences over which we have no control.

SPARKEION

Here far away from all the world,
Dissension and derision,
With Nature's wonders all unfurled
To our delighted vision,
With no one here
(At least in sight)
To interfere

With our delight,
And two fond lovers sever,
Oh do not free,
Thine hand from mine,
I swear to thee
My love is ever thine
For ever and for ever.

NICEMIS

On mountain top the air is keen,
And most exhilarating,
And we say things we do not mean
In moments less elating.
So please to wait
For thoughts that crop,
En tete-a-tete,
On mountain top,
May not exactly tally
With those that you
May entertain,
Returning to
The sober plain˙
Of yon relaxing valley

SPARKEION

Very well—if you won't have anything to say to me, I know who will.

NICEMIS

Who will?

SPARKEION

Daphne will.

NICEMIS

Daphne would flirt with anybody.

SPARKEION

Anybody would flirt with Daphne. She is quite as pretty as you and has twice as much back-hair.

NICEMIS

She has twice as much money, which may account for it.

SPARKEION

At all events, she has appreciation. She likes good looks.

NICEMIS

We all like what we haven;t got.

SPARKEION
She keeps her eyes open.

NICEMIS
Yes—one of them.

SPARKEION
Which one.

NICEMIS
The one she doesn't wink with.

SPARKEION
Well, I was engaged to her for six months and if she still makes eyes at me, you must attribute it to force of habit. Besides—remember—we are only half-married at present.

NICEMIS
I suppose you mean that you are going to treat me as shamefully as you treated her. Very well, break it off if you like. I shall not offer any objection. Thespis used to be very attentive to me. I'd just as soon be a manager's wife as a fifth-rate actor's.

[CHORUS heard, at first below, then enter DAPHNE, PRETTEIA, PREPOSTEROS, STUPIDAS, TIPSEION, CYMON, and other members of Thespis's company climbing over rocks at back. All carry small baskets.]

CHORUS [with dance]
Climbing over rocky mountain
Skipping rivulet and fountain,
Passing where the willows quiver
By the ever rolling river,
Swollen with the summer rain.
Threading long and leafy mazes,
Dotted with unnumbered daisies,
Scaling rough and rugged passes,
Climb the hearty lads and lasses,
Til the mountain-top they gain.

FIRST VOICE
Fill the cup and tread the measure
Make the most of fleeting leisure.
Hail it as a true ally
Though it perish bye and bye.

SECOND VOICE
Every moment brings a treasure
Of its own especial pleasure,
Though the moments quickly die,
Greet them gaily as they fly.

THIRD VOICE
Far away from grief and care,
High up in the mountain air,
Let us live and reign alone,
In a world that's all our own.

FOURTH VOICE
Here enthroned in the sky,
Far away from mortal eye,
We'll be gods and make decrees,
Those may honor them who please.

CHORUS
Fill the cup and tread the measure...etc.

[After CHORUS and COUPLES enter, THESPIS climbing over rocks]

THESPIS
Bless you, my people, bless you. Let the revels commence. After all, for thorough, unconstrained unconventional enjoyment give me a picnic.

PREPOSTEROS [very gloomily]
Give him a picnic, somebody.

THESPIS
Be quiet, Preposteros. Don't interrupt.

PREPOSTEROS
Ha. Ha. Shut up again. But no matter.

[STUPIDAS endeavors, in pantomime, to reconcile him. Throughout the scene PREPOSTEROS shows symptoms of breaking out into a furious passion, and STUPIDAS does all he can to pacify and restrain him.]

THESPIS
The best of a picnic is that everybody contributes what he pleases, and nobody knows what anybody else has brought til the last moment. Now, unpack everybody and let's see what there is for everybody.

NICEMIS
I have brought you—a bottle of soda water—for the claret-cup.

DAPHNE
I have brought you—lettuce for the lobster salad.

SPARKEION
A piece of ice—for the claret-cup.

PRETTEIA

A bottle of vinegar—for the lobster salad.

CYMON
A bunch of burrage for the claret-cup.

TIPSEION
A hard boiled egg—for the lobster salad.

STUPIDAS
One lump of sugar for the claret-cup.

PREPOSTEROS
He has brought one lump of sugar for the claret-cup? Ha.
Ha. Ha. [laughing melodramatically]

STUPIDAS
Well, Preposteros, what have you brought?

PREPOSTEROS
I have brought two lumps of the very best salt for the
lobster salad.

THESPIS
Oh—is that all?

PREPOSTEROS
All. Ha. Ha. He asks if it is all. {STUPIDAS consoles him]

THESPIS
But, I say—this is capital so far as it goes. Nothing could be better, but it doesn't go far enough. The claret, for instance. I don't insist on claret—or a lobster—I don't insist on lobster, but a lobster salad without a lobster, why it isn't lobster salad. Here, Tipseion.

TIPSEION [a very drunken, bloated fellow, dressed, however, with scrupulous accuracy and wearing a large medal around his neck]
My master.

[Falls on his knees to THESPIS and kisses his robe.]

THESPIS
Get up—don't be a fool. Where's the claret? We arranged last week that you were to see to that.

TIPSEION
True, dear master. But then I was a drunkard.

THESPIS
You were.

TIPSEION
You engaged me to play convivial parts on the strength of my personal appearance.

THESPIS
I did.

TIPSEION
Then you found that my habits interfered with my duties as low comedian.

THESPIS
True.

TIPSEION
You said yesterday that unless I took the pledge you would dismiss me from your company.

THESPIS
Quite so.

TIPSEION
Good. I have taken it. It is all I have taken since yesterday. My preserver. [Embraces him]

THESPIS
Yes, but where's the wine?

TIPSEION
I left it behind that I might not be tempted to violate my pledge.

PREPOSTEROS
Minion. [Attempts to get at him, is restrained by STUPIDAS]

THESPIS
Now, Preposteros, what is the matter with you?

PREPOSTEROS
It is enough that I am down-trodden in my profession. I will not submit to imposition out of it. It is enough that as your heavy villain I get the worst of it every night in a combat of six. I will not submit to insult in the day time. I have come out. Ha. Ha. to enjoy myself.

THESPIS
But look here, you know—virtue only triumphs at night from seven to ten—vice gets the best of it during the other twenty one hours. Won't that satisfy you? [STUPIDAS endeavours to pacify him.]

PREPOSTEROS [Irritated to STUPIDAS]
Ye are odious to my sight. Get out of it.

STUPIDAS [In great terror]
What have I done?

THESPIS
Now what is it. Preposteros, what is it?

PREPOSTEROS
I a — hate him and would have his life.

THESPIS [to STUPIDAS]
That's it—he hates you and would have your life. Now go and be merry.

STUPIDAS
Yes, but why does he hate me?

THESPIS
Oh—exactly. [To PREPOSTEROS] Why do you hate him?

PREPOSTEROS
Because he is a minion.

THESPIS
He hates you because you are a minion. It explains itself. Now go and enjoy yourselves. Ha. Ha. It is well for those who can laugh—let them do so—there is no extra charge. The light-hearted cup and the convivial jest for them—but for me—what is there for me?

SILLIMON
There is some claret-cup and lobster salad [handing some]

THESPIS [taking it]
Thank you. [Resuming] What is there for me but anxiety—ceaseless gnawing anxiety that tears at my very vitals and rends my peace of mind asunder? There is nothing whatever for me but anxiety of the nature I have just described. The charge of these thoughtless revellers is my unhappy lot. It is not a small charge, and it is rightly termed a lot because there are many. Oh why did the gods make me a manager?

SILLIMON [as guessing a riddle]
Why did the gods make him a manager?

SPARKEION
Why did the gods make him a manager.

DAPHNE
Why did the gods make him a manager?

PRETTEIA
Why did the gods make him a manager?

THESPIS
No—no—what are you talking about? What do you mean?

DAPHNE
I've got it—no don't tell us.

ALL
No—no—because—because

THESPIS [annoyed]
It isn't a conundrum. It's misanthropical question.

DAPHNE [Who is sitting with SPARKEION to the annoyance of NICEMIS who is crying alone]
I'm sure I don't know. We do not want you. Don't distress yourself on our account—we are getting on very comfortably—aren't we Sparkeion.

SPARKEION
We are so happy that we don't miss the lobster or the claret. What are lobster and claret compared with the society of those we love? [Embracing DAPHNE]

DAPHNE
Why, Nicemis, love, you are eating nothing. Aren't you happy dear?

NICEMIS [spitefully]
You are quite welcome to my share of everything. I intend to console myself with the society of my manager. [takes Thespis' arm affectionately].

THESPIS
Here I say—this won't do, you know—I can't allow it—at least before my company—besides, you are half-married to Sparkeion. Sparkeion, here's your half-wife impairing my influence before my company. Don't you know the story of the gentleman who undermined his influence by associating with his inferiors?

ALL
Yes, yes—we know it.

PREPOSTEROS [formally]
I do not know it. It's ever thus. Doomed to disappointment from my earliest years.

[STUPIDAS endeavours to console him]

THESPIS
There—that's enough. Preposteros—you shall hear it.

I once knew a chap who discharged a function
On the North South East West Diddlesex Junction.
He was conspicuous exceeding,
For his affable ways, and his easy breeding.
Although a chairman of directions,
He was hand in glove with the ticket inspectors.
He tipped the guards with brand new fivers,

And sang little songs to the engine drivers.
'Twas told to me with great compunction,
By one who had discharged with unction
A chairman of directors function
On the North South East West Diddlesex Junction.
Fol diddle, lol diddle, lol lol lay.

Each Christmas day he gave each stoker
A silver shovel and a golden poker.
He'd button holw flowers for the ticket sorters
And rich Bath-buns for the outside porters.
He'd moun the clerks on his first-class hunters,
And he build little villas for the road-side shunters,
And if any were fond of pigeon shooting,
He'd ask them down to his place at Tooting.
Twas told to me....etc.

In course of time there spread a rumour
That he did all this from a sense of humour.
So instead of signalling and stoking,
They gave themselves up to a course of joking.
Whenever they knew that he was riding,
They shunted his train on a lonely siding,
Or stopped all night in the middle of a tunnel,
On the plea that the boiler was a-coming through the funnel.
Twas told to me...etc.

It he wished to go to Perth or Stirling,
His train through several counties whirling,
Would set him down in a fit of larking,
At four a.m. in the wilds of Barking.
This pleased his whim and seemed to strike it,
But the general public did not like it.
The receipts fell, after a few repeatings,
And he got it hot at the annual meetings.
Twas told to me...etc.

He followed out his whim with vigour,
The shares went down to a nominal figure.
These are the sad results proceeding
From his affable ways and his easy breeding.
The line, with its rais and guards and peelers,
Was sold for a song to marine store dealers
The shareholders are all in the work'us,
And he sells pipe-lights in the Regent Circus.
Twas told to me...etc.

It's very hard. As a man I am naturally of an easy disposition. As a manager, I am compelled to hold myself aloof, that my influence may not be deteriorated. As a man I am inclined to fraternize with the pauper—as a manager I am compelled to walk around like this: Don't know yah. Don't know yah. Don't know yah.

[Strides haughtily about the stage. JUPITER, MARS, and APOLLO, in full Olympian costume appear on the three broken columns. THESPIANS scream.]

JUPITER, MARS, APOLLO
Presumptuous mortal.

THESPIS
Don't know ya. Don't know yah.

JUPITER, MARS, APOLLO [seated on broken pillars]
Presumptuous mortal.

THESPIS
I do not know you. I do not know you.

JUPITER, MARS, APOLLO
Presumptuous mortal.

THESPIS
Remove this person.

[STUPIDAS and PREPOSTEROS seize APOLLO and MARS]

JUPITER
Stop, you evidently don't know me. Allow me to offer you my card.

[Throws flash paper]

THESPIS
Ah yes, it's very pretty, but we don't want any at present. When we do our Christmas piece, I'll let you know. [Changing his manner] Look here, you know this is a private party and we haven't the pleasure of your acquaintance. There are a good many other mountains about, if you must have a mountain all to yourself. Don't make me let myself down before my company. [Resuming] Don't know yah, Don't know yah.

JUPITER
I am Jupiter, the king of the gods. This is Apollo. This is Mars.

[All kneel to them except THESPIS]

THESPIS
Oh. Then as I'm a respectable man, and rather particular about the company I keep, I think I'll go.

JUPITER

No—no—stop a bit. We want to consult you on a matter of great importance. There. Now we are alone. Who are you?

THESPIS

I am Thespis of the Thessalian Theatres.

JUPITER

The very man we want. Now as a judge of what the public likes are you impressed with my appearance as father of the gods?

THESPIS

Well to be candid with you, I am not. In fact I'm disappointed.

JUPITER

Disappointed?

THESPIS

Yes, you see you're so much out of repair. No, you don't come up to my idea of the part. Bless you, I've played you often.

JUPITER

You have.

THESPIS

To be sure I have.

JUPITER

And how have you dressed the part.

THESPIS

Fine commanding party in the prime of life. Thunderbolt—full beard—dignified manner—a good eal of this sort of thin "Don't know ya. Don't know yah. Don't know yah.

JUPITER [much affected]

I—I'm very much obliged to you. It's very good of you. I—I—I used to be like that. I can't tell you how much I feel it. And do you find I'm an impressive character to play?

THESPIS

Well no, I can't say you are. In fact we don't you you much out of burlesque.

JUPITER

Burlesque!

THESPIS

Yes, it's a painful subject, drop it, drop it. The fact is, you are not the gods you were—you're behind your age.

JUPITER
Well, but what are we to do? We feel that we ought to do something, but we don't know what.

THESPIS
Why don't you all go down to earth, incog, mingle with the world, hear and see what people think of you, and judge for yourselves as to the best means to take to restore your influence?

JUPITER
Ah, but what's to become of Olympus in the meantime?

THESPIS
Lor' bless you, don't distress yourself about that. I've a very good company, used to take long parts on the shortest notice. Invest us with your powers and we'll fill your places till you return.

JUPITER [aside]
The offer is tempting. But suppose you fail?

THESPIS
Fail. Oh, we never fail in our profession. We've nothing but great successes.

JUPITER
Then it's a bargain.

THESPIS
It's a bargain. [they shake hands on it]

JUPITER
And that you may not be entirely without assistance, we will leave you Mercury and whenever you find yourself in a difficulty you can consult him.

[Enter MERCURY]

JUPITER
So that's arranged—you take my place, my boy,
While we make trial of a new existence.
At length I will be able to enjoy
The pleasures I have envied from a distance.

MERCURY
Compelled upon Olympus here to stop,
While the other gods go down to play the hero.
Don't be surprised if on this mountain top
You find your Mercury is down at zero.

APOLLO
To earth away to join in mortal acts.
And gather fresh materials to write on.

Investigate more closely, several facts,
That I for centuries have thrown some light on.

DIANA
I, as the modest moon with crescent bow.
Have always shown a light to nightly scandal,
I must say I'd like to go below,
And find out if the game is worth the candle.

[Enter all thespians, summoned by MERCURY]

MERCURY
Here come your people.

THESPIS
People better now.

THESPIS
While mighty Jove goes down below
With all the other deities.
I fill his place and wear his "clo,"
The very part for me it is.
To mother earth to make a track,
They are all spurred and booted, too.
And you will fill, till they come back,
The parts you best are suited to.

CHORUS
Here's a pretty tale for future Iliads and Odysseys
Mortals are about to personate the gods and goddesses.
Now to set the world in order, we will work in unity.
Jupiter's perplexity is Thespis's opportunity.

SPARKEION
Phoebus am I, with golden ray,
The god of day, the god of day.
When shadowy night has held her sway,
I make the goddesses fly.
Tis mine the task to wake the world,
In slumber curled, in slumber curled.
By me her charms are all unfurled
The god of day am I.

CHORUS
The god of day, the god of day,
The park shall our Sparkeion play,
Ha Ha, etc.
The rarest fun and rarest fare

That ever fell to mortal share
Ha ha etc.

NICEMIS
I am the moon, the lamp of night.
I show a light — I show a light.
With radiant sheen I put to flight
The shadows of the sky.
By my fair rays, as you're aware,
Gay lovers swear—gay lovers swear,
While greybeards sleep away their care,
The lamp of night am I.

CHORUS
The lamp of night-the lamp of night.
Nicemis plays, to her delight.
Ha Ha Ha Ha.
The rarest fun and rarest fare,
That ever fell to mortal share,
Ha Ha Ha Ha

TIMIDON
Mighty old Mars, the god of war,
I'm destined for—I'm destined for.
A terribly famous conqueror,
With sword upon his thigh.
When armies meet with eager shout
And warlike rout, and warlike rout,
You'll find me there without a doubt.
The God of War am I.

CHORUS
The god of war, the god of war
Great Timidon is destined for.
Ha Ha Ha Ha
The rest fun and rarest fare
That ever fell to mortal share
Ha Ha Ha Ha

DAPHNE
When, as the fruit of warlike deeds,
The soldier bleed, the soldier bleeds,
Calliope crowns heroic deeds,
With immortality.
From mere oblivion I reclaim
The soldier's name, the soldier's name
And write it on the roll of fame,
The muse of fame am I.

CHORUS
The muse of fame, the muse of fame.
Callipe is Daphne's name.
Ha Ha Ha Ha
The rarest fun and rarest fare,
That ever fell to mortal share.
Ha Ha Ha Ha.

TUTTI
Here's a pretty tale.

[Enter procession of old GODS, they come down very much astonished at all they see, then passing by, ascent the platform that leads to the descent at the back.]

GODS
We will go,
Down below,
Revels rare,
We will share.
Ha Ha Ha
With a gay
Holiday
All unknown,
And alone
Ha Ha Ha.

TUTTI
Here's a pretty tale.

[The GODS, including those who have lately entered in procession group themselves on rising ground at back. The THESPIANS kneeling bid them farewell.]

ACT II

SCENE-the same scene as in Act I with the exception that in place of the ruins that filled the foreground of the stage, the interior of a magnificent temple is seen showing the background of the scene of Act I, through the columns of the portico at the back. High throne. L.U.E. Low seats below it. All the substitute gods and goddesses [that is to say, Thespians] are discovered grouped in picturesque attitudes about the stage, eating and drinking, and smoking and singing the following verses.

CHORUS
Of all symposia
The best by half
Upon Olympus, here await us.

We eat ambrosia.
And nectar quaff,
It cheers but don't inebriate us.
We know the fallacies,
Of human food
So please to pass Olympian rosy,
We built up palaces,
Where ruins stood,
And find them much more snug and cosy.

SILLIMON
To work and think, my dear,
Up here would be,
The height of conscientious folly.
So eat and drink, my dear,
I like to see,
Young people gay—young people jolly.
Olympian food my love,
I'll lay long odds,
Will please your lips—those rosy portals,
What is the good, my love
Of being gods,
If we must work like common mortals?

CHORUS
Of all symposia...etc.

[Exeunt all but NICEMIS, who is dressed as Diana and PRETTEIA, who is dressed as Venus. They take SILLIMON'S arm and bring him down]

SILLIMON
Bless their little hearts, I can refuse them nothing. As the Olympian stage-manager I ought to be strict with them and make them do their duty, but i can't. Bless their little hearts, when I see the pretty little craft come sailing up to me with a wheedling smile on their pretty little figure-heads, I can't turn my back on 'em. I'm all bow, though I'm sure I try to be stern.

PRETTEIA
You certainly are a dear old thing.

SILLIMON
She says I'm a dear old thing. Deputy Venus says I'm a dear old thing.

NICEMIS
It's her affectionate habit to describe everybody in those terms. I am more particular, but still even I am bound to admit that you are certainly a very dear old thing.

SILLIMON

Deputy Venus says I'm a dear old thing, and Deputy Diana who is much more particular, endorses it. Who could be severe with such deputy divinities.

PRETTEIA
Do you know, I'm going to ask you a favour.

SILLIMON
Venus is going to ask me a favour.

PRETTEIA
You see, I am Venus.

SILLIMON
No one who saw your face would doubt it.

NICEMIS [aside]
No one who knew her character would.

PRETTEIA
Well Venus, you know, is married to Mars.

SILLIMON
To Vulcan, my dear, to Vulcan. The exact connubial relation of the different gods and goddesses is a point on which we must be extremely particular.

PRETTEIA
I beg your pardon—Venus is married to Mars.

NICEMIS
If she isn't married to Mars, she ought to be.

SILLIMON
Then that decides it—call it married to Mars.

PRETTEIA
Married to Vulcan or married to Mars, what does it signify?

SILLIMON
My dear, it's a matter on which I have no personal feeling whatever.

PRETTEIA
So that she is married to someone.

SILLIMON
Exactly. So that she is married to someone. Call it married to Mars.

PRETTEIA

Now here's my difficulty. Presumptios takes the place of Mars, and Presumptios is my father.

SILLIMON
Then why object to Vulcan?

PRETTEIA
Because Vulcan is my grandfather.

SILLIMON
But, my dear, what an objection. You are playing a part till the real gods return. That's all. Whether you are supposed to be married to your father—or your grandfather, what does it matter? This passion for realism is the curse of the stage.

PRETTEIA
That's all very well, but I can't throw myself into a part that has already lasted a twelvemonth, when I have to make love to my father. It interferes with my conception of the characters. It spoils the part.

SILLIMON
Well, well. I'll see what can be done. [Exit PRETTEIA, L.U.E.) That's always the way with beginners, they've no imaginative power. A true artist ought to be superior to such considerations. [NICEMIS comes down R.] Well, Nicemis, I should say, Diana, what's wrong with you? Don't you like your part?

NICEMIS
Oh, immensely. It's great fun.

SILLIMON
Don't you find it lonely out by yourself all night?

NICEMIS
Oh, but I'm not alone all night.

SILLIMON
But, I don't want to ask any injudicious questions, but who accompanies you?

NICEMIS
Who? Why Sparkeion, of course.

SILLIMON
Sparkeion? Well, but Sparkeion is Phoebus Apollo [Enter SPARKEION] He's the sun, you know.

NICEMIS
Of course he is. I should catch my death of cold, in the night air, if he didn't accompany me.

SPARKEION
My dear Sillimon, it would never do for a young lady to be out alone all night. It wouldn't be respectable.

SILLIMON

There's a good deal of truth in that. But still—the sun—at night—I don't like the idea. The original Diana always went out alone.

NICEMIS
I hope the original Diana is no rule for me. After all, what does it matter?

SILLIMON
To be sure—what does it matter?

SPARKEION
The sun at night, or in the daytime.

SILLIMON
So that he shines. That's all that's necessary. [Exit NICEMIS, R.U.E.] But poor Daphne, what will she say to this.

SPARKEION
Oh, Daphne can console herself; young ladies soon get over this sort of thing. Did you never hear of the young lady who was engaged to Cousin Robin?

SILLIMON
Never.

SPARKEION
Then I'll sing it to you.

Little maid of Arcadee
Sat on Cousin Robin's knee,
Thought in form and face and limb,
Nobody could rival him.
He was brave and she was fair,
Truth they made a pretty paid.
Happy little maiden she—
Happy maid of Arcadee.

Moments fled as moments will
Happily enough, until
After, say, a month or two,
Robin did as Robins do.
Weary of his lover's play,
Jilted her and went away,
Wretched little maiden, she—
Wretched maid of Arcadee.

To her little home she crept,
There she sat her down and wept,
Maiden wept as maidens will—
Grew so thin and pale—until

Cousin Richard came to woo.
Then again the roses grew.
Happy little maiden she—
Happy maid of Arcadee.

[Exit SPARKEION]

SILLIMON
Well Mercury, my boy, you've had a year's experience of us here. How do we do it? I think we're rather an improvement on the original gods—don't you?

MERCURY
Well, you see, there's a good deal to be said on both sides of the question; you are certainly younger than the original gods, and, therefore, more active. On the other hand, they are certainly older than you, and have, therefore, more experience. On the whole I prefer you, because your mistakes amuse me.

Olympus is now in a terrible muddle,
The deputy deities all are at fault
They splutter and splash like a pig in a puddle
And dickens a one of 'em's earning his salt.
For Thespis as Jove is a terrible blunder,
Too nervous and timid—too easy and weak—
Whenever he's called on to lighten or thunder,
The thought of it keeps him awake for a week.

Then mighty Mars hasn't the pluck of a parrot.
When left in the dark he will quiver and quail;
And Vulcan has arms that would snap like a carrot,
Before he could drive in a tenpenny nail.
Then Venus's freckles are very repelling,
And Venus should not have a quint in her eyes;
The learned Minerva is weak in her spelling,
And scatters her h's all over the skies.

Then Pluto in kindhearted tenderness erring,
Can't make up his mind to let anyone die—
The Times has a paragraph ever recurring,
"Remarkable incidence of longevity."
On some it has some as a serious onus,
to others it's quite an advantage—in short,
While ev're life office declares a big bonus,
The poor undertakers are all in the court.

Then Cupid, the rascal, forgetting his trade is
To make men and women impartially smart,
Will only shoot at pretty young ladies,
And never takes aim at a bachelor's heart.

The results of this freak—or whatever you term it—
Should cover the wicked young scamp with disgrace,
While ev'ry young man is as shy as a hermit,
Young ladies are popping all over the place.

This wouldn't much matter—for bashful and shymen,
When skillfully handled are certain to fall,
But, alas, that determined young bachelor Hymen
Refuses to wed anybody at all.
He swears that Love's flame is the vilest of arsons,
And looks upon marriage as quite a mistake;
Now what in the world's to become of the parsons,
And what of the artist who sugars the cake?

In short, you will see from the facts that I'm showing,
The state of the case is exceedingly sad;
If Thespis's people go on as they're going,
Olympus will certainly go to the bad.
From Jupiter downward there isn't a dab in it,
All of 'em quibble and shuffle and shirk,
A premier in Downing Street forming a cabinet,
Couldn't find people less fit for their work.

[enter THESPIS L.U.E.]

THESPIS
Sillimon, you can retire.

SILLIMON
Sir, I—

THESPIS
Don't pretend you can't when I say you can. I've seen you do it—go.

[Exit SILLIMON bowing extravagantly. THESPIS imitates him]

Well, Mercury, I've been in power one year today.

MERCURY
One year today. How do you like ruling the world?

THESPIS
Like it. Why it's as straightforward as possible. Why there hasn't been a hitch of any kind since we came up here. Lor' the airs you gods and goddesses give yourselves are perfectly sickening. Why it's mere child's play.

MERCURY
Very simple isn't it?

THESPIS
Simple? Why I could do it on my head.

MERCURY
Ah—I darsay you will do it on your head very soon.

THESPIS
What do you mean by that, Mercury?

MERCURY
I mean that when you've turned the world quite topsy-turvy you won't know whether you're standing on your head or your heels.

THESPIS
Well, but Mercury, it's all right at present.

MERCURY
Oh yes—as far as we know.

THESPIS
Well, but, you know, we know as much as anybody knows; you know I believe the world's still going on.

MERCURY
Yes—as far as we can judge—much as usual.

THESPIS
Well, the, give the Father of the Drama his due Mercury.
Don't be envious of the Father of the Drama.

MERCURY
But you see you leave so much to accident.

THESPIS
Well, Mercury, if I do, it's my principle. I am an easy man, and I like to make things as pleasant as possible. What did I do the day we took office? Why I called the company together and I said to them: "Here we are, you know, gods and goddesses, no mistake about it, the real thing. Well, we have certain duties to discharge, let's discharge them intelligently. Don't let us be hampered by routine and red tape and precedent, let's set the original gods an example, and put a liberal interpretation on our duties. If it occurs to any one to try an experiment in his own department, let him try it, if he fails there's no harm done, if he succeeds it is a distinct gain to society. Don't hurry your work, do it slowly and well." And here we are after a twelvemonth and not a single complaint or a single petition has reached me.

MERCURY
No, not yet.

THESPIS
What do you mean by "no,not yet?"

MERCURY
Well, you see, you don't understand things. All the petitions that are addressed by men to Jupiter pass through my hands, and its my duty to collect them and present them once a year.

THESPIS
Oh, only once a year?

MERCURY
Only once a year—

THESPIS
And the year is up?

MERCURY
Today.

THESPIS
Oh, then I suppose there are some complaints?

MERCURY
Yes, there are some.

THESPIS [Disturbed]
Oh, perhaps there are a good many?

MERCURY
There are a good many.

THESPIS
Oh, perhaps there are a thundering lot?

MERCURY
There are a thundering lot.

THESPIS [very much disturbed]
Oh.

MERCURY
You see you've been taking it so very easy—and so have most of your company.

THESPIS
Oh, who has been taking it easy?

MERCURY
Well, all except those who have been trying experiments.

THESPIS

Well but I suppose the experiment are ingenious?

MERCURY
Yes; they are ingenious, but on the whole ill-judged. But it's time go and summon your court.

THESPIS
What for.

MERCURY
To hear the complaints. In five minutes they will be here.

[Exit]

THESPIS [very uneasy]
I don't know how it is, but there is something in that young man's manner that suggests that the father of the gods has been taking it too easy. Perhaps it would have been better if I hadn't given my company so much scope. I wonder what they've been doing. I think I will curtail their discretion, though none of them appear to have much of the article. It seems a pity to deprive 'em of what little they have.

[Enter DAPHNE, weeping]

THESPIS
Now then, Daphne, what's the matter with you?

DAPHNE
Well, you know how disgracefully Sparkeion—

THESPIS [correcting her]
Apollo—

DAPHNE
Apollo, then—has treated me. He promised to marry me years ago and now he's married to Nicemis.

THESPIS
Now look here. I can't go into that. You're in Olympus now and must behave accordingly. Drop your Daphne—assume your Calliope.

DAPHNE
Quite so. That's it. [mysteriously]

THESPIS
Oh—that is it? [puzzled]

DAPHNE
That is it. Thespis. I am Calliope, the muse of fame. Very good. This morning I was in the Olympian library and I took down the only book there. Here it is.

THESPIS [taking it]

Lempriere's Classical Dictionary. The Olympian Peerage.

DAPHNE
Open it at Apollo.

THESPIS [opens it]
It is done.

DAPHNE
Read.

THESPIS
"Apollo was several times married, among others to Issa, Bolina, Coronis, Chymene, Cyrene, Chione, Acacallis, and Calliope."

DAPHNE
And Calliope.

THESPIS [musing]
Ha. I didn't know he was married to them.

DAPHNE [severely]
Sir. This is the family edition.

THESPIS
Quite so.

DAPHNE
You couldn't expect a lady to read any other?

THESPIS
On no consideration. But in the original version—

DAPHNE
I go by the family edition.

THESPIS
Then by the family edition, Apollo is your husband.

[Enter NICEMIS and SPARKEION]

NICEMIS
Apollo your husband? He is my husband.

DAPHNE
I beg your pardon. He is my husband.

NICEMIS

Apollo is Sparkeion, and he's married to me.

DAPHNE
Sparkeion is Apollo, and he's married to me.

NICEMIS
He is my husband.

DAPHNE
He's your brother.

THESPIS
Look here, Apollo, whose husband are you? Don't let's have any row about it; whose husband are you?

SPARKEION
Upon my honor I don't know. I'm in a very delicate position, but I'll fall in with any arrangement Thespis may propose.

DAPHNE
I've just found out that he's my husband and yet he goes out every evening with that "thing."

THESPIS
Perhaps he's trying an experiment.

DAPHNE
I don't like my husband to make such experiments. The question is, who are we all and what is our relation to each other.

SPARKEION
You're Diana. I'm Apollo
And Calliope is she.

DAPHNE
He's your brother.

NICEMIS
You're another. He has fairly married me.

DAPHNE
By the rules of this fair spot
I'm his wife and you are not.

SPARKEION & DAPHNE
By the rules of this fair spot
I'm/she's his wife and you are not.

NICEMIS
By this golden wedding ring,

I'm his wife, and you're a "thing."

DAPHNE, NICEMIS, SPARKEION
By this golden wedding ring,
I'm/She's his wife and you're a "thing."

ALL
Please will someone kindly tell us.
Who are our respective kin?
All of us/them are very jealous
Neither of us/them will give in.

NICEMIS
He's my husband, I declare,
I espoused him properlee.

SPARKEION
That is true, for I was there,
And I saw her marry me.

DAPHNE
He's your brother—I'm his wife.
If we go by Lempriere.

SPARKEION
So she is, upon my life.
Really, that seems very fair.

NICEMIS
You're my husband and no other.

SPARKEION
That is true enough I swear.

DAPHNE
I'm his wife, and you're his brother.

SPARKEION
If we go by Lempriere.

NICEMIS
It will surely be unfair,
To decide by Lempriere. [crying]

DAPHNE
It will surely be quite fair,
To decide by Lempriere.

SPARKEION and THESPIS
How you settle it I don't care,
Leave it all to Lempriere.
[Spoken] The Verdict
As Sparkeion is Apollo,
Up in this Olympian clime,
Why, Nicemis, it will follow,
He's her husband, for the time. [indicating DAPHNE]

When Sparkeion turns to mortal
Join once more the sons of men.
He may take you to his portal [indicating NICEMIS]
He will be your husband then.
That oh that is my decision,
'Cording to my mental vision,
Put an end to all collision,
My decision, my decision.

ALL
That oh that is his decision. etc.

[Exeunt THESPIS, NICEMIS, SPARKEION and DAPHNE, SPARKEION with DAPHNE, NICEMIS weeping with
THESPIS. Mysterious music. Enter JUPITER, APOLLO and MARS from below, at the back of stage. All wear
cloaks, as disguise and all are masked]

JUPITER, APOLLO, MARS
Oh rage and fury, Oh shame and sorrow.
We'll be resuming our ranks tomorrow.
Since from Olympus we have departed,
We've been distracted and brokenhearted,
Oh wicked Thespis. Oh villain scurvy.
Through him Olympus is topsy turvy.
Compelled to silence to grin and bear it.
He's caused our sorrow, and he shall share it.
Where is the monster. Avenge his blunders.
He has awakened Olympian thunders.

[Enter MERCURY]

JUPITER
Oh monster.

APOLLO
Oh monster.

MARS
Oh monster.

MERCURY [in great terror]
Please sir, what have I done, sir?

JUPITER
What did we leave you behind for?

MERCURY
Please sir, that's the question I asked for when you went away.

JUPITER
Was it not that Thespis might consult you whenever he was in a difficulty?

MERCURY
Well, here I've been ready to be consulted, chockful of reliable information—running over with celestial maxims—advice gratis ten to four—after twelve ring the night bell in cases of emergency.

JUPITER
And hasn't he consulted you?

MERCURY
Not he—he disagrees with me about everything.

JUPITER
He must have misunderstood me. I told him to consult you whenever he was in a fix.

MERCURY
He must have though you said in-sult. Why whenever I opened my mouth he jumps down my throat. It isn't pleasant to have a fellow constantly jumping down your throat—especially when he always disagrees with you. It's just the sort of thing I can't digest.

JUPITER [in a rage]
Send him here. I'll talk to him.

[Enter THESPIS. He is much terrified]

JUPITER
Oh monster.

APOLLO
Oh monster.

MARS
Oh monster.

[THESPIS sings in great terror, which he endeavours to conceal]

JUPITER
Well sir, the year is up today.

APOLLO
And a nice mess you've made of it.

MARS
You've deranged the whole scheme of society.

THESPIS [aside]
There's going to be a row. [Aloud and very familiarly] My dear boy, I do assure you—

JUPITER
Be respectful.

APOLLO
Be respectful.

MARS.
Be respectful.

THESPIS
I don't know what you allude to. With the exception of getting our scene painter to "run up" this temple, because we found the ruins draughty, we haven't touched a thing.

JUPITER
Oh story teller.

APOLLO
Oh story teller.

MARS.
Oh story teller.

[Enter THESPIANS]

THESPIS
My dear fellows, you're distressing yourselves unnecessarily. The court of Olympus is about to assemble to listen to the complaints of the year, if any. But there are none, or next to none. Let the Olympians assemble.

[THESPIS takes chair. JUPITER, APOLLO, and MARS sit below him.

Ladies and gentlemen, it seems that it is usual for the gods to assemble once a year to listen to mortal petitions. It doesn't seem to me to be a good plan, as work is liable to accumulate; but as I am particularly anxious not to interfere with Olympian precedent, but to allow everything to go on as it has always been accustomed to go—why, we'll say no more about it. [aside] But how shall I account for your presence?

JUPITER

Say we are the gentlemen of the press.

THESPIS
That all our proceedings may be perfectly open and above-board I have communicated with the most influential members of the Athenian press, and I beg to introduce to your notice three of its most distinguished members. They bear marks emblematic of the anonymous character of modern journalism. [Business of introduction. Thespis is very uneasy] Now then, if you're all ready we will begin.

MERCURY [Brings tremendous bundle of petitions]
Here is the agenda.

THESPIS
What's that? The petitions?

MERCURY
Some of them. [Opens one and reads] Ah, I thought there'd be a row about it.

THESPIS
Why, what's wrong now?

MERCURY
Why, it's been a foggy Friday in November for the last six months and the Athenians are tired of it.

THESPIS
There's no pleasing some people. This craving for perpetual change is the curse of the country. Friday's a very nice day.

MERCURY
So it is, but a Friday six months long.—it gets monotonous.

JUPITER, APOLLO, MARS [rising]
It's perfectly ridiculous.

THESPIS [calling them]
Cymon.

CYMON [as time with the usual attributes]
Sir.

THESPIS [Introducing him to the three gods]
Allow me—Father Time—rather young at present but even time must have a beginning. In course of time, time will grow older. Now then, Father Time, what's this about a wet Friday in November for the last six months.

CYMON
Well, the fact is, I've been trying an experiment. Seven days in the week is an awkward number. It can't be halved. Two's into seven won't go.

THESPIS [tries it on his fingers]
Quite so—quite so.

CYMON
So I abolished Saturday.

JUPITER, APOLLO, MARS.
Oh but. [Rising]

THESPIS
Do be quiet. He's a very intelligent young man and knows what he is about. So you abolished Saturday. And how did you find it answer?

CYMON
Admirably.

THESPIS
 You hear? He found it answer admirably.

CYMON
Yes, only Sunday refused to take its place.

THESPIS
Sunday refused to take its place?

CYMON
Sunday comes after Saturday—Sunday won't go on duty after Friday. Sunday's principles are very strict. That's where my experiment sticks.

THESPIS
Well, but why November? Come, why November?

CYMON
December can't begin until November has finished. November can't finish because he's abolished Saturday. There again my experiment sticks.

THESPIS
Well, but why wet? Come now, why wet?

CYMON
Ah, that is your fault. You turned on the rain six months ago and you forgot to turn it off again.

JUPITER, APOLLO, MARS [rising]
On this is monstrous.

ALL
Order. Order.

THESPIS

Gentlemen, pray be seated. [to the others] The liberty of the press, one can't help it. [to the three gods] It is easily settled. Athens has had a wet Friday in November for the last six months. Let them have a blazing Tuesday in July for the next twelve.

JUPITER, APOLLO, MARS.

But—

ALL

Order. Order.

THESPIS

Now then, the next article.

MERCURY

Here's a petition from the Peace Society. They complain because there are no more battles.

MARS [springing up]

What.

THESPIS

Quiet there. Good dog—soho; Timidon.

TIMIDON [as Mars]

Here.

THESPIS

What's this about there being no battles?

TIMIDON

I've abolished battles; it's an experiment.

MARS [spring up]

Oh come, I say—

THESPIS

Quiet then. [To TIMIDON] Abolished battles?

TIMIDON

Yes, you told us on taking office to remember two things. To try experiments and to take it easy. I found I couldn't take it easy while there are any battles to attend to, so I tried the experiment and abolished battles. And then I took it easy. The Peace Society ought to be very much obliged to me.

THESPIS

Obliged to you. Why, confound it. Since battles have been abolished, war is universal.

TIMIDON

War is universal?

THESPIS
To be sure it is. Now that nations can't fight, no two of 'em are on speaking terms. The dread of fighting was the only thing that kept them civil to each other. Let battles be restored and peace reign supreme.

MERCURY
Here's a petition from the associated wine merchants of Mytilene? Are there no grapes this year?

THESPIS
Well, what's wrong with the associated wine merchants of Mytilene? Are there no grapes this year?

THESPIS
Plenty of grapes. More than usual.

THESPIS [to the GODS]
You observe, there is no deception. There are more than usual.

MERCURY
There are plenty of grapes, only they are full of ginger beer.

THREE GODS
Oh, come I say [rising they are put down by THESPIS]

THESPIS
Eh? what [much alarmed] Bacchus.

TIPSEION [as Bacchus]
Here.

THESPIS
There seems to be something unusual with the grapes of Mytilene. They only grow ginger beer.

TIPSEION
And a very good thing too.

THESPIS
It's very nice in its way but it is not what one looks for from grapes.

TIPSEION
Beloved master, a week before we came up here, you insisted on my taking the pledge. By so doing you rescued me from my otherwise inevitable misery. I cannot express my thanks. Embrace me. [Attempts to embrace him.]

THESPIS
Get out, don't be a fool. Look here, you know you're the god of wine.

TIPSEION
I am.

THESPIS [very angry]

Well, do you consider it consistent with your duty as the god of wine to make the grapes yield nothing but ginger beer?

TIPSEION

Do you consider it consistent with my duty as a total abstainer to grow anything stronger than ginger beer?

THESPIS

But your duty as the god of wine—

TIPSEION

In every respect in which my duty as the god of wine can be discharged consistently with my duty as a total abstainer, I will discharge it. But when the functions clash, everything must give way to the pledge. My preserver. [Attempts to embrace him]

THESPIS

Don't be a confounded fool. This can be arranged. We can't give over the wine this year, but at least we can improve the ginger beer. Let all the ginger beer be extracted from it immediately.

THREE GODS

We can't stand this,
We can't stand this.
It's much too strong.
We can't stand this.
It would be wrong.
Extremely wrong.
If we stood this.

If we stand this
If we stand this
We can't stand this.

DAPHNE, SPARKEION, NICEMIS

Great Jove, this interference.
Is more than we can stand;
Of them make a clearance,
With your majestic hand.

JUPITER

This cool audacity, it beats us hollow.
I'm Jupiter.

MARS

I'm Mars.

APOLLO

I'm Apollo.

[Enter DIANA and all the other GODS and GODDESSES.

ALL [kneeling with their foreheads on the ground]
Jupiter, Mars, and Apollo
Have quitted the dwellings of men;
The other gods quickly will follow.
And what will become of us then.
Oh pardon us, Jove and Apollo,
Pardon us, Jupiter, Mars:
Oh see us in misery wallow.
Cursing our terrible stars.

[Enter other GODS]

ALL THESPIANS
Let us remain, we beg of you pleadingly.

THREE GODS
Let them remain, they beg of us pleadingly.

THESPIS
Life on Olympus suits us exceedingly.

GODS
Life on Olympus suits them exceedingly.

THESPIS
Let us remain, we pray in humility.

GODS
Let 'em remain, they pray in humility.

THESPIS
 If we have shown some little ability.

GODS
If they have shown some little ability.
Let us remain, etc...

JUPITER
Enough, your reign is ended.
Upon this sacred hill.
Let him be apprehended
And learn out awful will.
Away to earth, contemptible comedians,
And hear our curse, before we set you free'

You shall be all be eminent tragedians,
Whom no one ever goes to see.

ALL
We go to earth, contemptible tragedians,
We hear his curse, before he sets us free,
We shall all be eminent tragedians,
Whom no one ever, ever goes to see.

SILLIMON SPARKEION, THESPIS
Whom no one
Ever goes to see.

[The THESPIANS are driven away by the gods, who group themselves in attitudes of triumph.]

THESPIS
Now, here you see the arrant folly
Of doing your best to make things jolly.
I've ruled the world like a chap in his senses,
Observe the terrible consequences.
Great Jupiter, whom nothing pleases,
Splutters and swears, and kicks up breezes,
And sends us home in a mood avengin'
In double quick time, like a railroad engine.
And this he does without compunction,
Because I have discharged with unction
A highly complicated function
Complying with his own injunction,
Fol, lol, lay

CHORUS
All this he does....etc.

[The GODS drive the thespians away. The THESPIANS prepare to descent the mountain as the curtain falls.

CURTAIN

W.S. Gilbert – A Short Biography

Sir William Schwenck Gilbert was born on November 18th, 1836 at 17 Southampton Street, Strand, London. His father, also named William, was a naval surgeon, who later became a writer of novels and short stories, some of which were illustrated by his son. Gilbert's mother was the former Anne Mary Bye Morris (1812–1888), the daughter of Thomas Morris, an apothecary.

Gilbert's parents were distant and stern, and there was no close bond between either themselves or their children (the marriage was to eventually break up in 1876). Gilbert had three younger sisters, Jane Morris, Anne Maude Mary Florence.

As a child, Gilbert was nicknamed "Bab".

The family travelled to Italy in 1838 and then France before finally returning to settle in London in 1847.

Gilbert was educated in Boulogne, France from age seven, then at Western Grammar School, Brompton, London, before the Great Ealing School, where he became head boy and wrote plays for school performances. He then attended King's College London, graduating in 1856.

His first thought for a career was to take examinations for a commission in the Royal Artillery, but the Crimean War had just ended and with fewer recruits needed only a commission in a line regiment was available. He opted instead for the Civil Service and was an assistant clerk in the Privy Council Office for four years. He hated it. In 1859 he joined the Militia, a part-time volunteer force, and served until 1878, as his other work allowed, and reached the rank of Captain.

To supplement his income Gilbert wrote a variety of stories, comic rants, theatre reviews (many in the form of a parody of the play being reviewed), and, using the pseudonym of his childhood nickname, "Bab" illustrated poems for several comic magazines, primarily Fun, started in 1861. His work was also published in the Cornhill Magazine, London Society, Tinsley's Magazine and Temple Bar. Gilbert was also the London correspondent for L'Invalide Russe and a drama critic for the Illustrated London Times. In the 1860s he also contributed to Tom Hood's Christmas annuals, to Saturday Night, the Comic News and the Savage Club Papers.

The poems, illustrated humorously by Gilbert, proved immensely popular and were reprinted in book form as the Bab Ballads. He would later return to many of these as source material for his plays and comic operas.

In 1863 he received a bequest of £300 allowing him to leave the civil service and attempt a career as a barrister. Unfortunately, he managed to attract few clients.

However, these events happily coincided with his first professionally produced play; Uncle Baby, which ran for seven weeks in the autumn of 1863.

In 1865–66, Gilbert collaborated with Charles Millward on several pantomimes, including Hush-a-Bye, Baby, On the Tree Top, or, Harlequin Fortunia, King Frog of Frog Island, and the Magic Toys of Lowther Arcade (1866).

Gilbert's first solo success, however, came a few days after Hush-a-Bye Baby premiered. His friend and mentor, Tom Robertson, was asked to deliver a pantomime within two weeks. Robertson couldn't and recommended Gilbert who took the job. Written and rushed to the stage in 10 days, Dulcamara, or the Little Duck and the Great Quack, a burlesque of Gaetano Donizetti's L'elisir d'amore, proved very popular. This led to a long series of further Gilbert opera burlesques, pantomimes and farces, full of dreadful puns, but showing signs of the satire that would later be such an integral part of Gilbert's work.

After a failed relationship with the novelist Annie Thomas, Gilbert married Lucy Agnes Turner, whom he affectionately called "Kitty", in 1867; she was 11 years his junior. They were socially active both in London and later at their new home at Grim's Dyke, often holding dinner parties. Although they had no children they had many pets, including several exotic ones.

Next followed Gilbert's biggest success so far; his penultimate operatic parody, Robert the Devil, a burlesque of Giacomo Meyerbeer's opera, Robert le diable, part of a triple bill that opened the Gaiety Theatre, London in 1868. It ran for over 100 nights.

In Victorian theatre, Gilbert's burlesques were considered very tasteful compared to the offerings of others. He would now move away from burlesque to plays with original plots and fewer puns. His first was An Old Score in 1869.

Theatre, at this time had fallen into disrepute. London was awash with poorly translated French operettas and cheaply written, prurient Victorian burlesques. From 1869 to 1875, Gilbert joined with Thomas German Reed (and his wife Priscilla), whose Gallery of Illustration sought to regain some of theatre's lost respect with family entertainments. This would be so successful that by 1885 Gilbert could safely state that original British plays were appropriate for an innocent 15-year-old girl to watch.

The initial work for the Gallery of Illustration, No Cards, was the first of six musical entertainments for the German Reeds, by Gilbert some with music composed by Thomas German Reed.

The German Reeds' intimate theatre allowed Gilbert to develop a personal style that would also cede to him control all aspects of production; set, costumes, direction and stage management.

Gilbert's first big hit at the Gallery of Illustration, Ages Ago, also opened in 1869. It marked the beginning of a collaboration with the composer Frederic Clay that would last seven years and cover four works. It was at a rehearsal for Ages Ago that Clay introduced Gilbert to Arthur Sullivan.

These musical works gave Gilbert a valuable education as a lyricist and he perfected the 'topsy-turvy' style that he had been developing in his Bab Ballads, where the humour was derived by setting up a ridiculous premise and following through on its logical consequences, however absurd they might be.

Ever busy he found time to create several 'fairy comedies' at the Haymarket Theatre. The premise was the idea of self-revelation by characters under the influence of magic or some supernatural experience. The first was The Palace of Truth (1870), based partly on a story by Madame de Genlis. In 1871, with Pygmalion and Galatea, one of seven plays that he produced that year, Gilbert scored his greatest hit to date. Together, these plays including The Wicked World (1873), Sweethearts (1874), and Broken Hearts (1875), did for Gilbert on the dramatic stage what the German Reed entertainments had done for him on the musical stage: they established that his talents were large and burgeoning, a writer of wide range, as comfortable with human drama as much as farcical humour.

Contemptorous with this period Gilbert pushed the satirical boundaries. He collaborated with Gilbert Arthur à Beckett on The Happy Land (1873), in part, a parody of his own The Wicked World, which was briefly banned because of its caricatures of Gladstone and his ministers. Similarly, The Realm of Joy (1873) was set in the lobby of a theatre performing a scandalous play (implied to be the Happy Land), with many jokes at the expense of the Lord Chamberlain (the "Lord High Disinfectant", as he's referred to in the play). In Charity (1874), however, Gilbert uses the freedom of the stage in a different way: to illuminate the contrasting ways in which society treated men and women who had sex outside of marriage. It was ground breaking and some see it as anticipating the 'problem plays' of Shaw and Ibsen.

Once established as a writer Gilbert was also the stage director, with strong, forceful opinions on how they should best be performed.

In Gilbert's 1874 burlesque, Rosencrantz and Guildenstern, the character Hamlet, in his speech to the players, sums up Gilbert's theory of comic acting: "I hold that there is no such antick fellow as your bombastical hero who doth so earnestly spout forth his folly as to make his hearers believe that he is unconscious of all incongruity". Again some say with this he prepared the ground for playwrights such as George Bernard Shaw and Oscar Wilde to be able to flourish.

Tom Robertson had "introduced Gilbert both to the revolutionary notion of disciplined rehearsals and to mise-en-scène or unity of style in the whole presentation – direction, design, music, acting." Like Robertson, Gilbert demanded discipline in his actors, that they know their lines, enunciate them clearly and keep to his stage directions, a new development for actors at the time. It also ushered in the replacement of the star with the disciplined ensemble.

Gilbert was meticulous in his preparations, making models of the stage and designing every action in advance. He refused to work with actors who challenged him. He was famous for demonstrating the action himself, even as he grew older. Such was his interest in standards that even during long runs and revivals, he closely supervised the performances of his plays, making sure that no one made additions or deletions.

Arthur Sullivan – A Short Biography

Sir Arthur Seymour Sullivan, MVO was born on May 13th 1842 in Lambeth, London. His father, Thomas Sullivan, a military bandmaster, clarinetist and music teacher, was born in Ireland and raised in Chelsea, London, and his mother, Mary Clementina (née Coghlan, English born, of Irish and Italian descent. Thomas Sullivan was based from 1845 to 1857 at the Royal Military College, Sandhurst, where he was the bandmaster and taught music privately to supplement his income. Young Sullivan became proficient with many of the instruments in the band and had composed an anthem, "By the waters of Babylon", by the age of eight. While proudly observing his son's obvious musical talent, he knew, at first hand, how insecure a profession it was and discouraged him from pursuing it.

Three years later whilst at a private school in Bayswater, Sullivan persuaded his parents and headmaster to allow him to apply for membership in the choir of the Chapel Royal. There were concerns that Sullivan at nearly 12 years of age was too old to be a treble as his voice would soon break. But he was accepted and soon became a soloist and, by 1856, was promoted to "first boy". Troublingly, even at this age, Sullivan's health was delicate, and he was easily fatigued.

However, Sullivan flourished under the training of the Reverend Thomas Helmore, and began to compose anthems and songs. Helmore arranged for one pieces, "O Israel", to be published in 1855.

In 1856, the Royal Academy of Music awarded the first Mendelssohn Scholarship to the 14-year-old Sullivan, granting him a year's training at the academy. His principal teacher there was John Goss, whose own teacher had been a pupil of Mozart. Initially Sullivan studied piano.

Sullivan's scholarship was extended to a second year, and then a third so that he could study in Germany, at the Leipzig Conservatoire. There he was trained in Mendelssohn's ideas and techniques as well as being exposed to Schubert, Verdi, Bach, and Wagner. Sullivan was an eager pupil and always looking for inspiration. On a visit to a synagogue, he was so struck by some of the cadences and progressions in the music that three decades later he would recall them for use in his serious opera, Ivanhoe.

Though the scholarship in Leipzig, was for one year he stayed for three. Sullivan credited his Leipzig period with rapid and sustained musical growth. His graduation piece, in 1861, was a set of incidental music to Shakespeare's The Tempest. Revised and expanded, it was performed at the Crystal Palace in 1862, a year after his return to London. It was an immediate sensation. He began building a reputation as England's most promising young composer.

He now embarked on composing with a series of ambitious works, interspersed with hymns, parlour songs and other light pieces of a more commercial nature. These compositions could not support him financially, and from 1861 to 1872 he supplemented his income working as a church organist, a task he enjoyed, and as a music teacher, sometimes at the Crystal Palace School, which he hated and gave up as soon as his finances allowed. Sullivan also took an early chance to compose pieces for royalty with the wedding of the Prince of Wales in 1863.

Sullivan began to put voice and orchestra together with The Masque at Kenilworth (Birmingham Festival, 1864). For Covent Garden that same year he composed his first ballet, L'Île Enchantée.

1865 saw Sullivan initiated into Freemasonry and was Grand Organist of the United Grand Lodge of England in 1887 during Queen Victoria's Golden Jubilee.

In 1866, he premiered his Irish Symphony and Cello Concerto, his only works in these genres. In the same year, his Overture in C (In Memoriam), commemorating the recent death of his father, was a commission from the Norwich Festival.

His overture Marmion was premiered by the Philharmonic Society in 1867. The Times called it "another step in advance on the part of the only composer of any remarkable promise that just at present we can boast."

Sadly, his initial attempt at opera, The Sapphire Necklace (1863–64) with a libretto by Henry F. Chorley, was not produced and, apart from the Overture and two songs published separately, is now lost.

His first surviving opera, Cox and Box (1866), was written for a private performance. It then received charity performances in London and Manchester, and was later produced at the Gallery of Illustration, where it ran for an extraordinary 264 performances. His soon to be partner, W. S. Gilbert, writing in Fun magazine, announced the score as superior to F. C. Burnand's libretto.

In 1867 Sullivan and Burnand were commissioned by Thomas German Reed for a two-act opera, The Contrabandista (revised and expanded as The Chieftain in 1894), but it was a much more modest success.

Sullivan wrote a group of seven part songs in 1868, the best-known of which is "The Long Day Closes". His last major work of the 1860s was a short oratorio, The Prodigal Son, which premiered in Worcester Cathedral as part of the 1869 Three Choirs Festival to much praise.

The Overture di Ballo, Sullivan's most enduring work, was composed for the Birmingham Festival in 1870.

1871 was a busy year. Sullivan published his only song cycle, The Window; or, The Songs of the Wrens, to words by Tennyson, and wrote the first of a series of suites of incidental music for West End productions of Shakespeare plays. Later in the year he composed a dramatic cantata, On Shore and Sea, for the opening of the London International Exhibition, and the beautiful hymn Onward, Christian Soldiers, with words by Sabine Baring-Gould. The Salvation Army adopted it and it has become one of Britain's best loved hymns.

Gilbert & Sullivan – The Collaboration Begins

In 1871, John Hollingshead commissioned Gilbert to work with Sullivan on a holiday piece for Christmas, entitled Thespis, or The Gods Grown Old, at the Gaiety Theatre. It was a success and its run was extended beyond the length of the Gaiety's normal run. And that seemed to be that.

Gilbert and Sullivan now went their separate ways. Gilbert worked again with Clay on Happy Arcadia (1872), and with Alfred Cellier on Topsyturveydom (1874), as well as several farces, operetta libretti, extravaganzas, fairy comedies, adaptations from novels, translations from the French. In 1874, he published his last piece for Fun magazine ("Rosencrantz and Guildenstern"), almost three years after his last and then promptly resigned citing disapproval of the new owner's other publishing interests.

Sullivan was busy on large-scale works in the early 1870s with the Festival Te Deum (Crystal Palace, 1872); and the oratorio, The Light of the World (Birmingham Festival, 1873). He also wrote suites of incidental music for productions of The Merry Wives of Windsor at the Gaiety in 1874 and Henry VIII at the Theatre Royal, Manchester in 1877 as well as continuing composing hymns.

In 1873, Sullivan had also contributed songs to Burnand's Christmas "drawing room extravaganza", The Miller and His Man.

By 1875 conditions were right for Gilbert and Sullivan to work together again. Back in 1868, Gilbert had published a short comedic libretto in Fun magazine entitled "Trial by Jury: An Operetta". In 1873, Gilbert had arranged with theatrical manager and composer, Carl Rosa, to expand this work into a one-act libretto. It was arranged that Rosa's wife was to sing the role of the plaintiff. Tragically, Rosa's wife died in childbirth in 1874. Gilbert offered the libretto to Richard D'Oyly Carte, but Carte could not use the piece at that time.

The project seemed grounded. A few months later Carte, was managing the Royalty Theatre, needed a short piece to pair with Offenbach's La Périchole. Carte had previously conducted Sullivan's Cox and Box and remembering that Gilbert had suggested a libretto to him, he reunited Gilbert and Sullivan. The result was the one-act comic opera Trial by Jury. Starring Sullivan's brother Fred as the Learned Judge, it became a surprise hit, as well as earning lavish praise from the critics. It played for over 300 performances in its first few seasons.

A short time after Trial had opened Sullivan wrote The Zoo, another one-act comic opera, with a libretto by B. C. Stephenson. It did not perform well. Now the path was clear for Gilbert & Sullivan to reteam together in earnest and dominate light opera for the next 15 years.

Light opera was not considered of much worth by serious critics. Gilbert wanted greater respect for himself and his profession. At that time plays were not published in a form suitable for a "gentleman's library", they were in the main cheap and unattractive in their look designed mainly for use by actors rather than the home reader. Gilbert now arranged in late 1875 for the publishers Chatto and Windus to print a volume of his plays in a format designed to appeal to the general reader, with an attractive binding and clear type, containing Gilbert's most respectable plays, including his most serious works, and mischievously capped off with Trial by Jury.

After the success of Trial by Jury, there were discussions towards reviving Thespis, but Gilbert and Sullivan were not able to agree on terms with Carte and his backers. The score to Thespis was never published, and tragically most of the music is now lost.

Carte took some time to gather together funds for another opera, and in this gap the ever-busy Gilbert produced several works including Tom Cobb (1875), Eyes and No Eyes (1875), and Princess Toto (1876), his last and most ambitious work with Clay, a three-act comic opera with full orchestra. He also found time to write two serious works, Broken Hearts (1875) and Dan'l Druce, Blacksmith (1876) and his most successful comic play, Engaged (1877), which inspired Oscar Wilde's The Importance of Being Earnest.

It was only by 1877 that Carte finally assembled enough investors to form the Comedy Opera Company with a mandate to launch a series of original English comic operas, beginning with a third collaboration between Gilbert and Sullivan, The Sorcerer, in November 1877.

The Sorcerer (1877), ran for 178 performances, a success by the standards of the day, but H.M.S. Pinafore (1878), which followed it, turned Gilbert and Sullivan into an international phenomenon. The bright and cheerful music of Pinafore was composed during a time when Sullivan was in the middle of a health scare. He was in terrible pain from a kidney stone. H.M.S. Pinafore ran for 571 performances in London, the then-second-longest theatrical run in history, it also gave birth to and more than 150 unauthorised productions in America alone. Although this increased the reach of their reputations it added nothing to their profits.

It was noted in the Times review of H.M.S. Pinafore that the opera was an early attempt at the establishment of a "national musical stage" ... free from risqué French "improprieties" and without the "aid" of Italian and German musical models.

As the profits rolled in came acrimony among the investors who felt the shares were unequal. One night the other Comedy Opera Company partners hired thugs to storm the theatre to steal the sets and costumes in order that they could mount a rival production. This was beaten off by stagehands and others at the theatre loyal to Carte. Carte was to now continue as sole impresario of the newly renamed D'Oyly Carte Opera Company.

For the next decade, the Savoy Operas were Gilbert's principal activity. The successful comic operas with Sullivan continued to appear every year or two, several of them being among the longest-running productions of the musical stage. After Pinafore came The Pirates of Penzance (1879), Patience (1881), Iolanthe (1882), Princess Ida (1884 and based on Gilbert's earlier farce, The Princess), The Mikado (1885), Ruddigore (1887), The Yeomen of the Guard (1888), and The Gondoliers (1889). Gilbert not only directed and oversaw all aspects of production, but he designed the costumes himself for Patience, Iolanthe, Princess Ida, and Ruddigore. He insisted on precise and authentic sets and costumes, which provided a foundation to ground and focus his absurd characters and situations.

In 1878, Gilbert realised a lifelong dream to play Harlequin, which he did at the Gaiety Theatre in an amateur charity production of The Forty Thieves, written partly by himself. Gilbert trained for Harlequin's stylised dancing with his friend John D'Auban, who had arranged the dances for some of his plays and would choreograph most of the Gilbert and Sullivan operas. Producer John Hollingshead later remembered, "the gem of the performance was the grimly earnest and determined Harlequin of W. S. Gilbert. It gave me an idea of what Oliver Cromwell would have made of the character."

In 1879, Sullivan suggested to a reporter from The New York Times the secret of his success with Gilbert: "His ideas are as suggestive for music as they are quaint and laughable. His numbers ... always give me musical ideas."

During this time, Gilbert and Sullivan also collaborated on one other major work. In 1880, Sullivan was appointed director of the triennial Leeds Music Festival. For his first festival he was commissioned to write a sacred choral work. He chose Henry Hart Milman's 1822 dramatic poem based on the life and death of Saint Margaret the Virgin for its basis. It premiered at the Leeds music festival in October 1880. Gilbert arranged the original epic poem by Henry Hart Milman into a libretto suitable for the music.

Carte opened the next Gilbert and Sullivan piece, Patience, in April 1881 at London's Opera Comique, where their past three operas had played. In October, Patience transferred to the new, larger, state-of-the-art (it was the first theatre to be lit entirely with electricity) Savoy Theatre, built with the profits of the previous Gilbert and Sullivan works.

From now on all of the partnership's collaborations were produced at the Savoy. The first to actually premiere here was Iolanthe in 1882, it was their fourth hit in a row.

Cracks were beginning to surface between the partners. Sullivan, despite the financial security, began to view his work with Gilbert as beneath his skills, as well as being repetitious. After Iolanthe, Sullivan had not intended to write a new work with Gilbert, but when his broker went bankrupt in late 1882 he suffered serious financial loss. Needs must and Sullivan buckled down to continue writing Savoy operas. In February 1883, he and Gilbert signed a five-year agreement with Carte, requiring them to produce a new comic opera on six months' notice.

The ever watchful Gilbert had the previous year installed a telephone in his home and another at the prompt desk at the Savoy Theatre, so that he could listen in on performances and rehearsals from his home study. Gilbert had referred to the new technology in Pinafore in 1878, only two years after the device was invented and before London even had telephones.

Better news arrived for Sullivan on May 22nd, 1883, when he was knighted by Queen Victoria for his "services ... rendered to the promotion of the art of music" in Britain. The musical establishment, and many critics, believed that this would put an end to his career as a composer of comic opera – that a musical knight should not stoop below oratorio or grand opera. But Sullivan having just signed the five-year agreement and the financial security that gave him could no nothing to change course now.

The next opera, Princess Ida in 1884, which was the duo's only three-act, blank verse work, stuttered. Its run was much shorter. Sullivan's score was praised but with box office receipts lagging in March 1884, Carte gave the six months' notice, under the partnership contract, requiring a new opera.

Sullivan's friend, composer Frederic Clay, had suffered a serious stroke in early December 1883 that ended his career at only 45 years of age. Sullivan, with his own longstanding kidney problems, and his desire to devote himself to more serious music, replied to Carte, "It is impossible for me to do another piece of the character of those already written by Gilbert and myself."

Gilbert however was already at work on it. His idea revolved around a plot in which people fell in love against their wills after taking a magic lozenge. Sullivan was unequoviacal in his response. On April 1st, 1884 he wrote that he had "come to the end of my tether with the operas. I have been continually keeping down the music in order that not one syllable should be lost.... I should like to set a story of human interest & probability where the humorous words would come in a humorous not serious situation, & where, if the situation were a tender or dramatic one the words would be of similar character."

There was now a lengthy exchange of correspondence in which Sullivan called Gilbert's plot sketch (particularly the "lozenge" element) unacceptably mechanical, and too similar in both its grotesque "elements of topsyturveydom" and in actual plot to their earlier work, especially The Sorcerer, and requested, time and again, that a new subject be found.

This impasse was finally resolved on May 8th when Gilbert proposed a plot that would be their most successful: The Mikado (1885). It was to run for a staggering 672 performances.

In 1886, Sullivan composed his last large-scale choral work of the decade. It was a cantata for the Leeds Festival, The Golden Legend, based on Longfellow's poem of the same name. Apart from the comic operas, this proved to be Sullivan's best received full-length work. It was given hundreds of performances during his lifetime alone.

Ruddigore followed The Mikado in 1887. It was profitable, but its nine-month run was deemed to be disappointing compared with the earlier Savoy operas.

Gilbert was always keen to use a good idea again and proposed for their next piece another version of the magic lozenge plot. It was immediately rejected by Sullivan. Gilbert finally proposed a quite serious opera, to which Sullivan was in agreement. Although not a grand opera, The Yeomen of the Guard (1888) gave him the opportunity to compose his most ambitious stage work to date. In 1885, Sullivan had told an interviewer, ""The opera of the future is a compromise (among the French, German and Italian schools) – a sort of eclectic school, a selection of the merits of each one. I myself will make an attempt to produce a grand opera of this new school. ... Yes, it will be an historical work, and it is the dream of my life."

After The Yeomen of the Guard opened, Sullivan turned once again to Shakespeare and composed incidental music for Henry Irving's production of Macbeth (1888).

Sullivan wished to produce further serious works with Gilbert. He had collaborated with no other librettist since 1875. Gilbert felt the reaction to The Yeomen of the Guard had "not been so convincing as to warrant us in assuming that the public want something more earnest still." Gilbert countered by proposing that Sullivan should go ahead with his plan to write a grand opera, as well as comic works for the Savoy. Sullivan was not immediately persuaded. He replied, "I have lost the liking for writing comic opera, and entertain very grave doubts as to my power of doing it."

Nevertheless, Sullivan soon commissioned a grand opera libretto from Julian Sturgis (the recommendation came from Gilbert), while suggesting to Gilbert that he revive an old idea for an opera set in colourful Venice. The comic opera was completed first in 1889. The Gondoliers has been described as a pinnacle of Sullivan's achievement. It was to be the last great Gilbert and Sullivan success.

In April 1890, during the run of The Gondoliers, Gilbert objected to Carte's financial accounts which included a charge to the partnership for the cost of new carpeting for the Savoy Theatre lobby. Gilbert believed that this was a maintenance expense that should be charged to Carte alone. Carte who was building a new theatre to present Sullivan's forthcoming grand opera was adamant that it was legitimate. Sullivan sided with Carte, even going so far as to testify erroneously as to certain old debts.

The partners were in fundamental disagreement and the relationship was for all intents and purposes ruptured.

Gilbert took legal action against Carte and Sullivan and refused to write a word more for the Savoy. Sullivan wrote to Gilbert in September 1890 that he was "physically and mentally ill over this wretched business. I have not yet got over the shock of seeing our names coupled ... in hostile antagonism over a few miserable pounds".

From Gilbert's point of view Carte had either made a series of serious blunders in the accounts, or deliberately attempted to swindle his partners.

Gilbert wrote to Sullivan on May 28th, 1891, a year after the end of the "Quarrel", that Carte had admitted "an unintentional overcharge of nearly £1,000 in the electric lighting accounts alone." It seemed to illustrate Gilbert's point.

Work beckoned for Gilbert and he got on with it. He wrote The Mountebanks with Alfred Cellier and then a flop Haste to the Wedding with George Grossmith. Sullivan wrote Haddon Hall with Sydney Grundy.

In the Courts Gilbert prevailed in the lawsuit and felt vindicated. Although there was acrimony and bitterness between them the partnership had been so profitable that, after the financial failure of the Royal English Opera House, Carte and his wife sought to reunite the author and composer.

In 1891, after numerous failed attempts at a reconciliation, Tom Chappell, the music publisher who printed the Gilbert and Sullivan operas, stepped in to mediate between his two most profitable artists, and within two weeks, against the odds, had succeeded. The result was to be two more operas: Utopia, Limited (1893) and The Grand Duke (1896).

A third was almost achieved when Gilbert offered a third libretto to Sullivan (His Excellency, 1894), but his insistence on casting Nancy McIntosh, his protegée from Utopia, led to Sullivan's refusal.

Utopia, was only a modest success, and The Grand Duke, in which a theatrical troupe, by means of a "statutory duel" and a conspiracy, takes political control of a grand duchy, was a failure.

The partnership now ended for good.

Graciously Gilbert would late write, "... Savoy opera was snuffed out by the deplorable death of my distinguished collaborator, Sir Arthur Sullivan. When that event occurred, I saw no one with whom I felt that I could work with satisfaction and success, and so I discontinued to write libretti."

WS Gilbert – Life After the Partnership

In 1889 Gilbert financed the building of the Garrick Theatre. The following year the Gilberts moved to Grim's Dyke in Harrow. In 1891, Gilbert was appointed Justice of the Peace for Middlesex. After casting Nancy McIntosh in Utopia, Limited, he and Lady Gilbert developed an affection for her, and she eventually gained the status of an unofficially adopted daughter, moving to Grim's Dyke to live with them. She continued living there, even after Gilbert's death, until Lady Gilbert's death in 1936.

Although Gilbert announced a retirement from the theatre after the poor initial run of his last work with Sullivan, The Grand Duke (1896) and the poor reception of his 1897 play The Fortune Hunter, he produced at least three more plays over the last dozen years of his life, including an unsuccessful opera, Fallen Fairies (1909), with Edward German.

Gilbert, as we know was very keen on keeping his plays in the shape they were originally intended and continued to supervise the various revivals of his works by the D'Oyly Carte Opera Company, including its London Repertory seasons in 1906–09.

The last play he wrote, The Hooligan, produced just four months before his death, is a study of a young condemned thug in a prison cell. Gilbert shows sympathy for his protagonist, the son of a thief who, brought up among thieves, kills his girlfriend.

This grim, yet powerful piece, became one of Gilbert's most successful serious dramas, and it is easy to see why many thought he was developing a new style only for death to rob of us of what would surely be a fascinating journey.

In these last years, Gilbert wrote children's book versions of H.M.S. Pinafore and The Mikado giving, in some cases, backstory that is not found in the librettos.

Official recognition for him came on July 15th, 1907 with his knighthood in recognition of his contributions to drama. Gilbert was the first British writer ever to receive a knighthood for his plays alone—earlier dramatist knights were knighted for political and other services.

On May 29th, 1911, Gilbert was about to give a swimming lesson to Winifred Isabel Emery and 17-year-old Ruby Preece in the lake of his home, Grim's Dyke, when Preece lost her footing and called for help. Gilbert dived in to save her but suffered a heart attack in the middle of the lake and died.

William Schwenck was cremated at Golders Green and his ashes buried at the Church of St. John the Evangelist, Stanmore. The inscription on Gilbert's memorial on the south wall of the Thames Embankment in London reads: "His Foe was Folly, and his Weapon Wit".

George Grossmith wrote to The Daily Telegraph that, although Gilbert had been described as an autocrat at rehearsals, "That was really only his manner when he was playing the part of stage director at rehearsals. As a matter of fact, he was a generous, kind true gentleman, and I use the word in the purest and original sense."

Gilbert's legacy, aside from building the Garrick Theatre are the canon of Savoy Operas and other works that are either still being performed or in print all these years later. He has made a lasting and defining influence on both the American and British musical theatre. The innovations in content and form of the works that he and Sullivan developed, and in Gilbert's theories of acting and stage direction, directly influenced the development of the modern musical throughout the 20th century. Gilbert's lyrics use punning, as well as complex internal and two and three-syllable rhyme schemes, and served as a model for such 20th century Broadway lyricists as P.G. Wodehouse, Cole Porter, Ira Gershwin, and Lorenz Hart.

Gilbert's influence on the English language has also been marked, with well-known phrases such as "A policeman's lot is not a happy one", "short, sharp shock", "What never? Well, hardly ever!", and "let the punishment fit the crime" arising from his pen.

Arthur Sullivan – Life After the Partnership

Sullivan's only grand opera, Ivanhoe, based on Walter Scott's novel, opened at Carte's new Royal English Opera House on January 31st, 1891. Sullivan completed the score too late to meet Carte's planned production date, and costs had overrun to such an extent that Carte insisted on a contractual penalty of £3,000 for the delay. However, when it opened it ran 155 consecutive performances, a wonderful run for a serious opera, and garnered good reviews. Afterwards, Carte was unable to fill the new opera house with other productions, and, unfairly, Ivanhoe was blamed for the failure of the opera house.

Later in 1891, New York beckoned for Sullivan and his music for Tennyson's The Foresters, which ran at Daly's Theatre in New York in 1892, but failed in London the following year.

Sullivan returned to comic opera, but needed a new collaborator. His next piece was Haddon Hall in 1892, with a libretto by Sydney Grundy based somewhat loosely on the elopement of Dorothy Vernon with John Manners. Although still comic, the tone and style of the work was more serious and romantic than the operas with Gilbert. It nonetheless enjoyed a run of 204 performances, and earned critical praise.

In 1894 Sullivan teamed up again with F. C. Burnand for The Chieftain, a heavily-reworked version of their earlier two-act opera, The Contrabandista, alas it failed.

The following year Sullivan provided incidental music for the Lyceum, this time for J. Comyns Carr's King Arthur.

As we know Gilbert and Sullivan did reunite for The Grand Duke in 1896. But it failed and they never worked together again. This did not affect the constant revival of their earlier operas at the Savoy.

In May 1897, Sullivan's full-length ballet, Victoria and Merrie England, opened at the Alhambra Theatre in celebration of the Queen's Diamond Jubilee. The work's seven scenes celebrate English history and culture, with the Victorian period as the grand finale. It ran for six months which was a great achievement. Following this was The Beauty Stone in 1898, with a libretto by Arthur Wing Pinero and J. Comyns Carr. Based on mediaeval morality plays the opera was a critical failure and, on the whole, a commercial failure running for only seven weeks.

Success came in 1899, to benefit "the wives and children of soldiers and sailors" on active service in the Boer War, when Sullivan composed the music of a jingoistic song, "The Absent-Minded Beggar", to a text by Rudyard Kipling. It was a sensation and raised a staggering £250,000 from performances and the sale of sheet music and other merchandise. Later that year he returned to his comic roots with In The Rose of Persia, with a libretto by Basil Hood overlapping a setting of exotic Arabian Nights with plot elements of The Mikado. It was well received, and, apart from those with Gilbert, was his most successful full-length collaboration. Another opera with Hood, The Emerald Isle, quickly went into preparation, but sadly Sullivan died before it completion.

On November 22nd, 1900 Arthur Seymour Sullivan died of heart failure, following an attack of bronchitis, at his flat in London. The unfinished opera, The Emerald Isle, was completed by Edward German and premiered in 1901. His Te Deum Laudamus, written to commemorate the end of the Boer War, was performed posthumously.

Sullivan wished to be buried in Brompton Cemetery with his parents and brother, but by order of the Queen he was buried in St. Paul's Cathedral. In addition to his knighthood, honours awarded to Sullivan in his lifetime included Doctor in Music, honoris causa, by the universities of Cambridge (1876) and Oxford (1879); Chevalier, Légion d'honneur, France (1878); The Order of the Medjidieh conferred by the Sultan of Turkey (1888); and appointment as a Member of the Fourth Class of the Royal Victorian Order (MVO) in 1897.

In all, Sullivan's artistic output included 23 operas, 13 major orchestral works, eight choral works and oratorios, two ballets, one song cycle, incidental music to several plays, numerous hymns and other church pieces, and a large body of songs, parlour ballads, part songs, carols, and piano and chamber pieces.

Although Sullivan had several long term affairs and was also known to have a roving eye that led him to frequent liaisons with many other women he never married.

Rachel Scott Russell was the first of his great loves. Her parents' disapproval meant they met secretly but by 1868, Sullivan was enmeshed in a simultaneous and secret affair with Rachel's sister Louise. Both relationships had ceased by early 1869.

Sullivan's affair with the American socialite, Fanny Ronalds, a woman three years his senior, who had two children began when they met in Paris around 1867. The affair began in earnest soon after she moved to London in 1871. Despite his wandering ways she was a constant companion up to the time of Sullivan's death, but around 1889 or 1890, the sexual relationship seems to have ended.

In 1896, the 54-year-old Sullivan proposed marriage to 22-year-old Violet Beddington but she refused.

The favourite playgrounds for Sullivan were Paris and the south of France, with friends ranging from European royalty to Claude Debussy, and where the casinos enabled him to indulge his passion for gambling.

Sullivan enjoyed playing tennis although, according to George Grossmith, "I have seen some bad lawn-tennis players in my time, but I never saw anyone so bad as Arthur Sullivan".

He was devoted to his parents, particularly his mother, until her death in 1882. Henry Lytton wrote, "I believe there was never a more affectionate tie than that which existed between Sullivan and his mother, a very witty old lady, and one who took an exceptional pride in her son's accomplishments.

Sullivan once explained his method of working; "I don't use the piano in composition – that would limit me terribly". Sullivan explained that he did not wait for inspiration, but had "to dig for it. ... I decide on the rhythm before I come to the question of melody. ... I mark out the metre in dots and dashes, and not until I have quite settled on the rhythm do I proceed to actual notation."

In composing the Savoy operas, Sullivan wrote the vocal lines of the musical numbers first, and these were given to the actors. He, or an assistant, improvised a piano accompaniment at the early rehearsals; he wrote the orchestrations later, after he had seen what Gilbert's stage business would be. He left the overtures until last and often delegated their composition, based on his outlines, to his assistants, often adding his suggestions or corrections. Those Sullivan wrote himself include Thespis, Iolanthe, Princess Ida, The Yeomen of the Guard, The Gondoliers, The Grand Duke and probably Utopia Limited. Most of the overtures are structured as a potpourri of tunes from the operas in three sections: fast, slow and fast. The overtures from the Gilbert and Sullivan operas remain popular. Sullivan invariably conducted the operas on their opening nights.

In general, Sullivan preferred to write in major keys. In the Savoy operas less than 5% of the numbers are in a minor key and even in his serious works the major prevails. Sullivan was happy on occasion to use chords traditionally considered technically incorrect. When reproached for using consecutive fifths in Cox and Box, he replied "if 5ths turn up it doesn't matter, so long as there is no offence to the ear."

Sullivan's orchestra for the Savoy Operas was typical of any other pit orchestra of his era: 2 flutes (+ piccolo), oboe, 2 clarinets, bassoon, 2 horns, 2 cornets, 2 trombones, timpani, percussion and strings. According to Geoffrey Toye, the number of players in the Savoy orchestra was originally 31. Sullivan argued hard for an increase in the pit orchestra's size, and starting with The Yeomen of the Guard, the orchestra was augmented with a second bassoon and a bass trombone. Sullivan generally orchestrated each score at almost the last moment, noting that the accompaniment for an opera had to wait until he saw the staging, so that he could judge how heavily or lightly to orchestrate each part of the music. For his large-scale orchestral pieces, Sullivan added a second oboe part, sometimes double bassoon and bass clarinet, more horns, trumpets, tuba, and sometimes an organ and/or a harp. Many of these pieces used very large orchestras.

Sullivan's critical reputation has undergone extreme changes since he first came to prominence in the 1860s. At first, critics were struck by his potential, and he was hailed as the long-awaited great English composer. His incidental music to The Tempest received an acclaimed premiere at the Crystal Palace just before Sullivan's 20th birthday in April 1862. The Athenaeum wrote:

When Sullivan turned to comic opera with Gilbert, the serious critics began to express disapproval. Peter Gammond writes of "misapprehensions and prejudices, delivered to our door by the Victorian firm Musical Snobs Ltd. ... frivolity and high spirits were sincerely seen as elements that could not be exhibited by anyone who was to be admitted to the sanctified society of Art." As early as 1877 The Figaro wrote that Sullivan "has all the ability to make him a great composer, but he wilfully throws his opportunity away. ... He possesses all the natural ability to have given us an English opera, and, instead, he affords us a little more-or-less excellent fooling." Few critics denied the excellence of Sullivan's theatre scores. The Theatre wrote that "Iolanthe sustains Dr Sullivan's reputation as the most spontaneous, fertile, and scholarly composer of comic opera this country has ever produced." However, comic opera, no matter how skilfully crafted, was viewed as an intrinsically lower form of art than oratorio. The Athenaeum's review of The Martyr of Antioch declared: "It is an advantage to have the composer of H.M.S. Pinafore occupying himself with a worthier form of art."

Although the more solemn members of the musical establishment could not forgive Sullivan for writing music that was both comic and accessible, he was, nevertheless, "the nation's de facto composer laureate".

Gilbert & Sullivan – A Concise Bibliography

The Collaborative Pieces

All of these operas are full-length two-act works, except for Trial by Jury, which is in one act, and Princess Ida, which is three acts.

Thespis (1871)
Trial by Jury (1875)
The Sorcerer (1877)
H.M.S. Pinafore (1878)
The Pirates of Penzance (1879)
Patience (1881)
Iolanthe (1882)
Princess Ida (1884)
The Mikado (1885)
Ruddigore (1887)
The Yeomen of the Guard (1888)
The Gondoliers (1889)
Utopia, Limited (1893)
The Grand Duke (1896)

Poetry

The Bab Ballads, a collection of comic verse published roughly between 1865 and 1871
Songs of a Savoyard, London, 1890, a collection of Gilbert's song lyrics.

Short Stories

Foggerty's Fairy & Other Tales, a collection of short stories and essays, mainly from before 1874.

Some other short stories but not in the above appear here:-

Belgravia, Vol. 2 (1867). "From St. Paul's to Piccadilly," pp. 67–74
Fun, Vol. 1 new series (1865-1866) (several contributions by Gilbert; near end of volume)
Fun Christmas Number 1865, ("The Astounding Adventure of Wheeler J. Calamity,")
London Society, Vol. 13 (1868) (three "Thumbnail Sketches" by Gilbert)
On the Cards: Routledge's Christmas Annual (1867) ("Diamonds," and "The Converted Clown,")

Other Books

The Pinafore Picture Book, 1908, retelling the story of H.M.S. Pinafore for children, in prose narrative
The Story of The Mikado, 1921, a similar retelling of The Mikado for children

Plays and Musical Stage Works
Selected stage works that were important to Gilbert's career or were otherwise notable, in chronological order, excluding those listed under other headings below:

Dulcamara, or the Little Duck and the Great Quack (1866)
La Vivandière (1867)
Harlequin Cock Robin and Jenny Wren (1867), a Christmas pantomime.
The Merry Zingara (1868)
Robert the Devil (1868), it opened the Gaiety Theatre, London and ran in the provinces for 3 years.
The Pretty Druidess (1869), a parody of Norma – the last of Gilbert's five "operatic burlesques"
An Old Score (1869) (rewritten as "Quits!" in 1872) Gilbert's first full-length comedy.
The Princess (1870). Musical farce; the precursor to Princess Ida.
The Palace of Truth (1870).
Creatures of Impulse (1871), music by Alberto Randegger. From Gilberts story "A Strange Old Lady".
Pygmalion and Galatea (1871).
Randall's Thumb (1871). A comedy that opened the Royal Court Theatre.
The Wicked World (1873).
The Happy Land (1873). This work was briefly banned for its sharp satire of government ministers.
The Realm of Joy (1873).
The Wedding March (1873) a farce adapted from Un Chapeau de Paille d'Italie.
Rosencrantz & Guildenstern (published 1874, performed 1891). Gilbert's burlesque of Hamlet.
Charity (1874). Concerns Victorian attitudes towards sex outside of marriage.
Sweethearts (1874).

Tom Cobb (1875).
Broken Hearts (1875). The last of Gilbert's "fairy comedies", this was one of Gilbert's favourite plays.
Dan'l Druce, Blacksmith (1876).
Engaged (1877).
The Ne'er-do-Weel (1878); rewritten as "The Vagabond" after a few weeks.
The Forty Thieves (1878). Co-written with three other writers, WSG played Harlequin.
Gretchen (1879)
Foggerty's Fairy (1881)
Brantinghame Hall (1888) Gilbert's biggest flop, it sent producer Rutland Barrington into bankruptcy.
The Fortune Hunter (1897). Its reception provoked WSG to announce retiring from writing for the stage.
The Fairy's Dilemma (1904).
The Hooligan (1911).

German Reed Entertainments
Gilbert wrote six one-act musical entertainments for the German Reeds between 1869 and 1875. They were successful in their own right and also helped form Gilbert's mature style as a dramatist.

No Cards (1869)
Ages Ago (1869). Gilbert's first collaboration with Frederic Clay, ran for 350 performances.
Our Island Home (1870)
A Sensation Novel (1871)
Happy Arcadia (1872)
Eyes and No Eyes (1875)

Early Comic Operas
The Gentleman in Black (1870; music by Frederic Clay). The score is lost.
Les Brigands (1871), an English adaptation of Jacques Offenbach's operetta.
Topsyturveydom (1874; music by Alfred Cellier). The score is lost.
Princess Toto (1876; music by Frederic Clay). A three-act opera.

Later Operas (Without Sullivan)
Though not as popular as the works with Arthur Sullivan, a few of Gilbert's later works arguably have stronger plots than the last two Gilbert and Sullivan operas.

The Mountebanks (1892; music; Alfred Cellier). This is the "lozenge plot" that Sullivan declined to set on several occasions.
Haste to the Wedding (1892; music; George Grossmith). An unsuccessful adaptation of The Wedding March.
His Excellency (1894; music; Osmond Carr). Gilbert felt that if Sullivan had set it, the piece would have been "another Mikado".
Fallen Fairies (1909; music by Edward German). Gilbert's last opera, which was a failure.

Parlour Ballads
The Yarn of the Nancy Bell, with music by Alfred Plumpton. One of the Bab Ballads. 1869.

Thady O'Flynn, with music by James L. Molloy. 1868. From No Cards.
Would You Know that Maiden Fair, with music by Frederic Clay. From Ages Ago. c. 1869.
Corisande, with music by James L. Molloy. 1870.
Eily's Reason, with music by James L. Molloy. 1871.
Three songs from A Sensation Novel: "The Detective's Song", "The Tyrannical Bridegroom", and "The Jewel". 1871
The Distant Shore, with music by Arthur Sullivan. 1874.
The Love that Loves me Not, with music by Arthur Sullivan. 1875.
Sweethearts, with music by Arthur Sullivan. 1875.
Let Me Stay, with music by Walter Maynard. 1875.

Arthur Sullivan – His Other Works

Operas
The Sapphire Necklace (ca. 1863; unperformed)
Cox and Box (1866)
The Contrabandista (1867)
The Zoo (1875)
Ivanhoe (1891)
Haddon Hall (1892)
The Chieftain (1894)
The Beauty Stone (1898)
The Rose of Persia (1899)
The Emerald Isle (1901; completed by Edward German)

Incidental Music to Plays
The Tempest (1861)
The Merchant of Venice (1871)
The Merry Wives of Windsor (1874)
Henry VIII (1877)
Macbeth (1888)
Tennyson's The Foresters (1892)
J. Comyns Carr's King Arthur for Henry Irving (1895)

Sheet Music

Ballets and Song Cycle
L'Île Enchantée (1864 ballet)
Victoria and Merrie England (1897 ballet)
The Window; or, The Song of the Wrens (1871 song cycle)

Choral Works with Orchestra
The Masque at Kenilworth (1864)

The Prodigal Son (Sullivan) (1869)
On Shore and Sea (1871)
Festival Te Deum (1872)
The Light of the World (Sullivan) (1873)
The Martyr of Antioch (1880)
Ode for the Opening of the Colonial and Indian Exhibition (1886)
The Golden Legend (1886)
Ode for the Laying of the Foundation Stone of The Imperial Institute (1887)
Te Deum Laudamus (1902; performed posthumously)

Orchestral Works
Overture in D (1858; now lost)
Overture The Feast of Roses (1860; now lost)
Procession March (1863)
Princess of Wales's March (1863)
Symphony in E, "Irish" (1866)
Overture in C, "In Memoriam" (1866)
Concerto for Cello and Orchestra (1866)
Overture Marmion (1867)
Overture di Ballo (1870)
Imperial March (1893)
The Absent-Minded Beggar March (1899)

Other Works

Songs & Parlour Ballads
Absent-minded Beggar (Rudyard Kipling) 1899
Arabian Love Song (Percy Bysshe Shelley) 1866
Ay de mi, My Bird (George Eliot)1874
Bid me at least Goodbye (Sydney Grundy) 1894
Birds in the Night (Lionel H. Lewin) 1869
Bride from the North (Henry F. Chorley) 1863
Care is all Fiddle-dee-dee (F. C. Burnand) 1874
Chorister, The (Fred. E. Weatherly) 1876
Christmas Bells at Sea (C. L. Kenney) 1875
County Guy (Walter Scott) 1867
Distant Shore, The (W. S. Gilbert) 1874
Dove Song (William Brough) 1869
E tu nol sai - see You Sleep (G. Mazzucato) 1889
Edward Gray (Alfred Tennyson)(1880
Ever (Mrs Bloomfield Moore) 1887
First Departure - see The Chorister (Rev. E. Munroe) 1874
Give (Adelaide Anne Procter) 1867
Golden Days (Lionel H. Lewin)1872
Guinevere! (Lionel H. Lewin) 1872
I Heard the Nightingale (Rev. C. H. Townsend) 1863

I Wish to Tune my Quiv'ring Lyre (Anacreon; trans. Lord Byron) 1868
I Would I were a King (Victor Hugo; trans. A. Cockburn) 1878
Ich möchte hinaus es jauchzen (A. Corrodi) 1859
If Doughty Deeds (Robert Graham of Gartmore) 1866
In the Summers Long Ago (J. P. Douglas) 1867
Let Me Dream Again (B. C. Stephenson) 1875
Lied, mit Thränen halbgeschrieben (Eichendorff)1861
Life that Lives for You (Lionel H. Lewin) 1870
Little Darling Sleep Again (Cradle Song) (anon) 1874
Living Poems (H. W. Longfellow)1874
Longing for Home (Jean Ingelow) 1904
Looking Back (Louisa Gray)1870
Looking Forward (Louisa Gray) 1873
Lost Chord, The (Adelaide Anne Procter) 1877
Love that Loves Me Not, The (W. S. Gilbert) 1875
Maiden's Story, The (Emma Embury) 1867
Marquis de Mincepie, The (F. C. Burnand) 1874
Mary Morison (Robert Burns) 1874
Moon in Silent Brightness, The (Bishop Reginald Heber) 1868
Mother's Dream, The (Rev. W. Barnes) 1868
My Dear and Only Love (Marquis of Montrose) 1874
My Dearest Heart (anon) 1874
My Heart is like a Silent Lute (Benjamin Disraeli) 1904
My Love - see "There Sits a Bird in Yonder Tree
My Love Beyond the Sea - see "In the Summers Long Ago"
None but I Can Say (Lionel H. Lewin)1872
O Fair Dove, O Fond Dove (Jean Ingelow) 1868
O Israel (Hosea) 1855
O Mistress Mine (William Shakespeare) 1866
O Swallow, Swallow (Alfred Tennyson) 1900
Oh Sweet and Fair (A. F. C. K.) 1868
Oh! bella mia - see "Oh! Ma Charmante"
Oh! Ma Charmante (Victor Hugo) 1872
Old Love Letters (S. K. Cowen) 1879
Once Again (Lionel H. Lewin) 1872
Orpheus with his Lute (William Shakespeare) 1866
River, The (anon) 1875
Roads Should Blossom, The (anon) 1864
Rosalind (William Shakespeare) 1866
Sad Memories (C. J. Rowe) 1869
Sailor's Grave, The (H. F. Lyte) 1872
St. Agnes' Eve (Alfred Tennyson) 1879
Shadow, A. (Adelaide Anne Procter)1886
She is not Fair to Outward View (Hartley Coleridge) 1866
Sigh no More, Ladies (William Shakespeare) 1866
Sleep My Love, Sleep (R. Whyte Melville) 1874
Snow Lies White, The (Jean Ingelow) 1868
Sometimes (Lady Lindsay of Balcarres) 1877

Sweet Day So Cool (George Herbert) 1864
Sweet Dreamer - see "Oh! Ma Charmante"
Sweethearts (W. S. Gilbert) 1875
Tears, Idle Tears (Alfred Tennyson) 1900
Tender and True (Dinah Maria Mulock) 1874
There Sits a Bird on Yonder TreeRev. (C. H. Barham) 1873
Thou art Lost to Me (anon) 1865
Thou art Weary (Adelaide Anne Procter) 1874
Thou'rt Passing Hence (Felicia Hemans) 1875
To One in Paradise (Edgar Allan Poe) 1904
Troubadour, The (Walter Scott) 1869
Village Chimes, The (C. J. Rowe) 1870
Weary Lot is Thine, Fair Maid, A (Walter Scott) 1866
We've Ploughed our Land (anon)1875
When Thou Art Near (W. J. Stewart) 1877
White Plume, The - see "The Bride from the North"
Will He Come? (Adelaide A. Procter) 1865
Willow Song, The (William Shakespeare)1866
You Sleep (B. C. Stephenson) 1889

Hymns (Title & First Line)

Adoro Te - Saviour, again to Thy dear name we raise (Arranger)
All This Night - All this night bright angels sing
Angel Voices - Angel voices, ever singing
Audite Audientes me - I heard the voice of Jesus say
Bethlehem - While shepherd's watched their flocks (Arranger)
Bishopgarth - O King of Kings, Whose reign of old
Bolwell - Thou to whom the sick and dying
Carrow - My God, I thank Thee Who has made
Chapel Royal - O love that wilt not let me go
Christus - Show me not only Jesus dying
Clarence - Winter reigneth o'er the land
Coena Domini - Draw nigh, and take the body of the Lord
Come Unto Me - Come unto Me, ye weary (Arranger)
Constance - I've found a Friend; oh, such a Friend
Coronae - Crown Him, with many crowns
Courage, Brother - Courage, brother, do not stumble
Dominion Hymn - God bless our wide dominion
Dulce Sonans - Angel voices, ever singing
Ecclesia - The church has waited long
Ellers - Saviour, again to Thy dear name we raise (Arranger)
Evelyn - In the hour of my distress
Ever Faithful - Let us with a gladsome mind
Fatherland (St. Edmund) - I'm but a stranger here
Formosa (Falfield) - Love Divine, all love excelling
Fortunatus - Welcome, happy morning!
Golden Sheaves - To Thee, O Lord, our hearts we raise

Hanford - Jesu, my Saviour, look on me
Heber (Gennesareth) - When through the torn sail
Holy City - Sing Alleluia forth in duteous praise
Hushed was the Evening Hymn - Hushed was the evening hymn
Hymn of the Homeland - The homeland, the homeland
Lacrymae - Lord, in this Thy mercy's day
Leominster - A few more years shall roll (Arranger)
Light - Holy Spirit! Come in might! (Arranger)
Litany (1) - Jesu, life of those who die
Litany (2) - Jesu, we are far away
Long Home, The - Tender Shepherd, Thou hast still'd
Lux eoi - All is bright and cheeful round us
Lux in Tenebris - Lead, kindly Light
Lux Mundi - O Jesu, Thou art standing
Marlborough - O Strength and Stay, upholding all creation (Arranger)
Mount Zion - Rock of Ages, cleft for me
Nearer Home - For ever with the Lord (Arranger)
Noel - It came upon the midnight clear (Arranger)
Old 137th - Great King of nations, hear our prayer (Arranger)
Paradise - O Paradise!
Parting - With the sweet word of peace (Arranger)
Pilgrimage - From Egypt's bondage come
Promissio Patris - Our blest Redeemer, ere He breathed
Propior Deo - Nearer, my God, to Thee
Rest - Art thou weary, art thou languid
Resurrexit - Christ is risen!
Roseate Hues, The - The roseate hues of early dawn
Safe Home - Safe home, safe home in port
St. Ann - The Son of God goes forth to war (Arranger)
St. Francis - O Father, who hast created all
St. Gertrude - Onward, Christian soldiers
St. Kevin - Come, ye faithful, raise the strain
St. Lucian - Of Thy love some gracious token
St. Luke (St. Nathaniel) - God moves in a mysterious way
St. Mary Magdalene - Saviour, when in dust to Thee
St. Millicent - Let no tears to-day be shed
St. Patrick - He is gone - a cloud of light
St. Theresa - Brightly gleams our banner
Saints of God - The Saints of God, their conflict past.
Springtime - For all Thy love and goodness (Arranger)
Strain Upraise, The - The Strain upraise in joy and praise
Thou God of Love - Thou God of Love, beneath Thy sheltering wing
Ultor Omnipotens - God the all terrible! King who ordainest
Valete - Sweet Saviour, bless us 'ere we go
Veni, Creator - Come Holy Ghost, our souls inspire
Victoria - To mourn our dead we gather here

The term "Part Song" is more usually applied to one where the highest part carries the melody with the other voices supplying the accompanying harmonies.

Also included here are the soprano duet, The Sisters, and the trio Sullivan composed for the play Olivia by W. G. Wills, Morn, Happy Morn.

O Lady Dear (Madrigal) - Composed 1857, unpublished.
It was a Lover and his Lass - Words by Shakespeare. Performed at the Royal Academy of Music, 1857, unpublished.
Seaside Thoughts - Words by Bernard Bartram. Composed 1857. Published 1904.
The Last Night of the Year - Words by H. F. Chorley. Published 1863.
O Hush Thee, My Babie - Words by Walter Scott. Published 1867.
The Rainy Day - Words by H. W. Longfellow. Published 1867.
Evening - Words by Lord Houghton, after Goethe. Published 1868.
Parting Gleams - Words by Aubrey de Vere. Published 1868.
Echoes - Words by Thomas Moore. Published 1868.
The Long Day Closes - Words by H. F. Chorley. Published 1868.
Joy to the Victors - Words by Walter Scott. Published 1868
The Beleaguered - Words by H. F. Chorley. Published 1868.
It Came Upon the Midnight Clear - Words by E. H. Sears. Published 1871.
Lead, Kindly Light - Words by J. H. Newman. Published 1871.
Through Sorrows Path - Words by H. Kirke White. Published 1871.
Say, Watchman, What of the Night? - Words from Isaiah. Published 1871.
The Way is Long and Dreary - Words by Adelaide Anne Procter. Published 1871.
Morn, Happy Morn - Composed for the play, Olivia by W. G. Wills. Published 1878.
The Sisters - Words by Alfred Tennyson. Published 1881.
Wreaths for our Graves - Words by L. F. Massey. Published 1898.
Fair Daffodils - Words by Robert Herrick. Published 1904.

By the Waters of Babylon - Composed c. 1850. Unpublished.
Sing unto the Lord - Composed 1855. Unpublished.
Psalm 103 - Composed 1856. Unpublished.
We have heard with our ears
(i) Dedicated to Sir George Smart and performed at the Chapel Royal, January 1860.
(ii) Dedicated to Rev. Thomas Helmore. 1865.
O Love the Lord - Dedicated to John Goss. 1864.
Te Deum, Jubilate, Kyrie (in D major) 1866.
O God, Thou art Worthy - Composed for the wedding of Adrian Hope, 3 June 1867. Published in 1871.
O Taste and See - Dedicated to Rev. C. H. Haweis. 1867.
Rejoice in the Lord - Composed for the wedding of Rev. R. Brown-Borthwick, 16 April 1868.
Sing, O Heavens - Dedicated to Rev. F. C. Byng. 1869.
I Will Worship - Dedicated to Rev. F. Gore Ouseley. 1871.
Two Choruses adapted from Russian Church Music, 1874.
(i) Turn Thee Again

(ii) Mercy and Truth
I Will Mention Thy Loving-kindness - Dedicated to John Stainer. 1875.
I Will Sing of Thy Power. 1877.
Hearken Unto Me, My People. 1877.
Turn Thy Face. 1878.
Who is Like unto Thee - Dedicated to Walter Parratt. 1883.
I Will Lay Me Down in Peace - Composed 1868. Published only in 1910.

Christmas Carols & Songs

Advent

Hearken unto me, my people - An Anthem for Advent or General Use. Words from Isaiah. (1877)

Christmas Carols

All this night bright angels sing - Words by W. Austin. (1870)
I Sing the Birth - Words by Ben Jonson. (1868)
It Came Upon the Midnight Clear - Words by E. H. Sears.
Part Song for Soprano Solo and Choir (1871)
Hymn Tune "Noel" (1874)
Upon the Snow-clad Earth (1876)
While Shepherds Watched - Words by Nahum Tate (1874)
Hark! What Mean those Holy Voices? - Words by John Cawood (1883)

Songs

Christmas Bells at Sea - Words by Charles Kenney (1875)
Two songs from The Miller and His Man - A Christmas Drawing Room Entertainment. Words by F. C. Burnand (1874)
The Marquis de Mincepie
Care is all Fiddle-dee-dee
The Last Night of the Year - Part Song - Words by H. F. Chorley (1863)

Chamber Music & Solo Piano
Scherzo - Piano Solo, 1857, unpublished.
Capriccio No. 2 - Piano Solo (unfinished), 1857, unpublished.
String Quartet - Performed at Leipzig, May 1859. Published 2000
Romance in G minor - For string quartet, 1859. Published 1964.
Thoughts - Two pieces for piano solo, Published by Cramer, 1862.
An Idyll - For Cello and Piano. Composed in 1865 and Published 1899.
Allegro Risoluto - Piano solo, 1866. Published only in 1974
Berceuse - Based on the theme of Hushed was the Bacon from Cox and Box but with additional material.
Day Dreams - Six pieces for piano solo. 1867
Duo Concertante - Cello and piano. 1868
Twilight - Piano solo. 1868

www.ingramcontent.com/pod-product-compliance
Lightning Source LLC
Chambersburg PA
CBHW060049050426
42448CB00011B/2368